Supernatural Fiction
for Teens

SUPERNATURAL FICTION FOR TEENS

500 Good Paperbacks to Read for Wonderment, Fear, and Fun

COSETTE KIES

Chair and Professor
Department of Library and Information Studies
Northern Illinois University
DeKalb, Illinois

1987
LIBRARIES UNLIMITED, INC.
Littleton, Colorado

LIBRARIES UNLIMITED, INC.
P.O. Box 263
Littleton, Colorado 80160-0263

Library of Congress Cataloging-in-Publication Data

Kies, Cosette N., 1936-
  Supernatural fiction for teens.

  Includes indexes.
  1. Young adult fiction--Bibliography.
  2. Supernatural in literature--Bibliography.
  3. Paperbacks--Bibliography. 4. Bibliography--
Best books--Young adult fiction. 5. Bibliography--
Best books--Fantastic fiction. 6. Fantastic fiction--
Bibliography. I. Title.
Z1037.K485 1987   [PN1009.A1]   016.80883'937   87-3228
ISBN 0-87287-602-0

Libraries Unlimited books are bound with Type II nonwoven material that
meets and exceeds National Association of State Textbook Administrators'
Type II nonwoven material specifications Class A through E.

Contents

7152377

Foreword

Young people have many enthusiasms, and the strange, the unexplained, and supernatural occurrences are high among them. Their fascination is partially satisfied and partially stimulated as they see and hear and read more in these areas of interest. Anyone who has visited high school libraries where books on the occult are kept at the desk or in some other special area knows this happens primarily because supply can scarcely keep up with demand. Busy librarians and teachers do not always have the time, opportunity, or inclination to inform themselves about good books to read about the supernatural, nor to make the connections between films for this audience and the books on which they were based. Cosette Kies has prepared this bibliography for all of them—the young adults and the adults who want to help them.

Kies's competence as a bibliographer has been proved in earlier publications. Her enthusiasm for the subject informs the work she presents here. Readers who want books by the same author, books related to films they've enjoyed, or books on similar themes can use this bibliography independently and make many choices based on the readable annotations and accompanying lists. Librarians, teachers, and booksellers may consider the bibliography a useful tool for selection of titles, but when they are not using it themselves, they should be sure it is accessible to the young adults for whom it can be a key to further wonderment, fear, and fun.

Peggy Sullivan

Introduction

The supernatural encompasses a fascinating range of subjects, most of which are intriguing themes for fiction. Teenagers, like other readers, have shown great interest in reading supernatural fiction in recent years, and a considerable amount of material is available at the present time.

Very simply defined, the supernatural includes all subjects not explainable in terms of present-day science. In this particular compilation of titles for teens, the supernatural is organized in three categories with three major thrusts: (1) those areas now included in parapsychology and psychic phenomena, such as ghosts and haunted houses, reincarnation, altered states of consciousness, levitation, time travel, fortune-telling, faith healing, and alchemy; (2) tales and legends with strong magical and occult elements from various cultures, such as Arthurian tales, lost lands, Heaven and Hell, eternal life, fairy tales, mythical beasts, shamanism, astrology, voodoo, good versus evil, and witchcraft and satanism; and (3) horror, both traditional and modern, from the supernatural gothic fiction tradition, which emphasizes the terrors of the heart, to vampires and werewolves, curses, science gone wrong, transformation, and monsters of all sorts. Works of pure fantasy are not included unless authors have based their works heavily on traditional mythic and/or occult themes. Science fiction, sword and sorcery, alternative (parallel) worlds, animals endowed with human attributes, and futurism are not included.

Fictional works based on these fascinating themes provide all readers, including teens, with speculative books which excite, tantalize, amaze, and horrify. The wide range of subjects and explorations provides a rich body of literature to share with teens, and almost any reader could find something appealing in this listing. The listing is not an attempt to provide only the highest quality, although some very fine pieces of writing are represented. Instead, the intent has been to give an idea of the various works available, from the humor of *Mad Magazine* through "grossed-out" horror books full of violence and disgusting descriptions, to gentle stories of ghostly maidens and a few classics that sometimes even teens will read. In the end, quality in this area is probably a very subjective judgment to be made by the teens themselves. Their interests are very likely to be piqued by what seems possible and real to them. They are not likely to analyze horror fiction, such as that written by Stephen King, in terms of literary criticism, yet they will sense the excellent pacing of King's work, for that is what makes his stories move along and keeps the reader eagerly scanning the pages. The archaic writing style employed by nineteenth-century authors will not necessarily turn teens off; instead, they may secretly like these works because they give the impression of being old, arcane mysteries of some sort—because the books are written in the fashion of an earlier time, the supernatural becomes somehow more believable.

Four types of books are listed in the main body of the text: (1) books written specifically for teens; (2) books written for younger teens that may appeal to readers of high interest/low reading level books; (3) books written for adults, including, in many cases, explicit sex, gore, violence, and vulgar language; and (4) books now considered to be classics. A letter designating the category is to be found in each entry following the bibliographic information, as follows:

A   Written for teens

B   Written for younger teens

C   Written for adults

D   Classic

Selections were made somewhat subjectively. Some works judged to be unlikely to appeal to today's teens, such as works by James Branch Cabell, were omitted. An attempt was made to include some new talents, as well as leading contemporary and classic authors. Because of the wide range of reading abilities and cultural sophistication of teens, books for younger teens include a few titles which might be considered more appropriate for younger readers. It is difficult to categorize books in the supernatural, for paperback publishers are currently engaging in a sort of "cross-publishing," taking books originally published for children and reissuing them in adult paperback format to appeal to the popular fantasy market. On the other hand are books written for adults, including a number of titles in the horror genre. Books beyond the American experience are included in order to provide a sense of the rich traditions of the supernatural in other cultures.

Availability of specific titles is always a problem, particularly with paperbacks, since books may go out-of-print quickly. In the area of the supernatural, however, high interest and brisk sales seem to keep some titles in-print longer, and some titles are reissued, usually with a new cover design. Certain subjects and themes seem to be immensely popular at present, such as the legend of King Arthur, and many books are available on the story of Camelot. By keeping abreast of such trends, the wise librarian is able to stock up in certain areas, while continuing to seek out worthy titles on less popular subjects.

In the following lists of 500 supernatural fiction titles for teens, a unique item number precedes the author's name. Pseudonyms, such as Mark Twain and Saki, have been used if the author's name appears that way on the books. The author's real name is noted in parentheses. Following the author's name is the title. The paperback imprint for the book follows, including place of publication, publisher, year of publication, number of pages and ISBN (if available). Following in parentheses is a note on the original publication of the title. So that it will stand out for quick reference, the code follows the bibliographic information, in boldface type. Information about the series and/or sequels appears on a separate line. Following are other works by the same author which might also appeal to teen readers. If a film has been based on the book, brief information regarding it is given. This is done also for titles which are novelizations of movie scripts. Each entry includes a brief annotation of the book title, suitable for use in booklists. Contents of short story collections are listed as well. The final piece of information is a note on the subject, given in square brackets. Whenever possible, the most specific subject headings have been used. For example, the head "Arthurian legends" is used for books about Camelot, rather than the broader term, "Legends, Christian."

The compilation is meant to have multiple uses. First and foremost, of course, it is meant to serve as a purchasing guide for librarians and teens, and second as a reading guide. It may also be used for programming, selecting films to show through the movie list and finding book titles for booktalks in the subject index.

Overall, this guide is meant to help librarians and teens find the books of interest to them in the field of supernatural fiction. A good source for keeping current with books and movies (through advertisements, reviews, and interviews with authors and movie directors) likely to be of interest to teens is the magazine *Rod Serling's The Twilight Zone*.

Additional reference sources are available for avid readers. These include:

1. Everett Bleiler, **The Guide to Supernatural Fiction**. Kent, Ohio: Kent State University Press, 1983.

A survey of over 7,000 stories and books on the supernatural published between 1750 and 1960.

2. Everett Bleiler, ed., **Supernatural Fiction Writers: Fantasy and Horror**. New York: Scribner's, 1985. 2 vols.

A survey of over 140 major authors in the supernatural field. Each entry includes an essay about the author and his or her development and works.

3. Stephen King, **Danse Macabre**. New York: Everest House, 1981.

An exploration of the appeal of horror by the best-selling author and former English teacher.

4. Baird Searles, Beth Meacham, and Michael Franklin, **A Reader's Guide to Fantasy**. New York: Avon, 1982.

A series of entries dealing mostly with contemporary writers of fantasy. Some useful material in the appendix includes books in series and thematic indexes.

5. Jack Sullivan, ed., **The Penguin Encyclopedia of Horror and the Supernatural**. New York: Viking Penguin, 1986.

A compilation of over 600 shorter entries and 50 essays dealing with authors, illustrators, movie makers and stars, critics, television programs, and media involved in the production of supernatural entertainment.

6. Marshall Tymn, **Horror Literature: A Core Collection and Reference Guide**. New York: Bowker, 1981.

A source book to horror literature with emphasis on its earlier years. Covers authors, books, periodicals, associations, poetry, awards, criticism, and reference sources.

7. Marshall Tymn, Kenneth Zahorski, and Robert Boyer, **Fantasy Literature: A Core Collection and Reference Guide**. New York: Bowker,
   1979.

   Similar in format and coverage to the Tymn *Horror Literature.*

As with any book of this sort, thanks are due to many people. Ralene
Linneman assisted with the bibliographic checking. Peggy Sullivan wrote the
foreword and did some copyediting, as did Loretta Rielly. Finally, I owe my
thanks to my colleagues at Northern Illinois University and elsewhere for their
interest and moral support.

Part 1
Supernatural Paperback Fiction for Teens

1. Aaron, Chester. **Out of Sight, Out of Mind.** New York: Bantam, 1986. 181pp. ISBN 0-553-26027-8. (First published by Lippincott, 1982). **B**

Twins with ESP powers, Erin and Sean, find themselves in a dangerous international episode when they try to deliver a speech vital to world peace. Their parents had been originally scheduled to give the speech, but they were killed by terrorists. Now the terrorists want Erin and Sean out of the way as well. [Paranormal abilities]

Aaron, Sidney. *See* Chayefsky, Paddy.

2. Adams, Richard. **The Girl in a Swing.** New York: Signet, 1980. 371pp. ISBN 0-451-13467-2. (First published by Knopf, 1980). **C**
   Other works: *Maia; The Plague Dogs; Shardak; Watership Down.*

Alan Desland, an English dealer in porcelain, tries to ignore his talent for ESP. When he meets the beautiful, bewitching Kathe, he finds his self-made, logical world slipping away. [Ghosts; Paranormal abilities; Reincarnation]

3. Adler, C. S. **Footsteps on the Stairs.** New York: Dell, 1984. 160pp. ISBN 0-440-42654-5. (First published by Delacorte, 1982). **B**

Plump Dodie finds her new life in an old house on the salt marsh with a reserved new stepsister complicated by the mysterious presence of two ghosts, sisters from an earlier time. [Ghosts]

4. Aiken, Joan. **A Touch of Chill.** London: Fontana Lions, 1981. 190pp. ISBN 0-006-71764-0. (First published by Victor Gollancz, 1979). **A**
   Other works: *Up the Chimney Down; A Bundle of Chill; All but a Few.*

Scary stories by the daughter of poet Conrad Aiken include "Lodgers," "Mrs. Considine," "The Sewanee Glide," "Listening," "The Companion," "The Rented Swan," "Jugged Hare," "A Game of Black and White," "Time to Laugh," " 'He': The Story about Caruso," "The Helper," "Power-cut," "Who Goes down This Dark Road?" "A Train Full of War-Lords." [Short stories]

5. Aiken, Joan. **A Whisper in the Night.** London: Fontana Lions, 1983. 189pp. ISBN 0-00-672133-8. (First published by Victor Gollancz, 1982). **A**

Delightfully shivery stories for teens include "Old Fillikin," "Miss Spitfire," "She Was Afraid of Upstairs," "The Birthday Party," "The Black Cliffs," "Finders Keepers," "The Hunchback of Brook Green," "Mrs. Chatterbox," "Sultan: A Friend," "Hanging Matter," "Picnic Area," "Merminister," "The Swan Child." [Short stories]

6. Alcock, Vivien. **Ghostly Companions**. London: Fontana Lions, 1985. 124pp. ISBN 0-00-672535-X. (First published by Methuen, 1984). **A** Other works: *The Haunting of Cassie Palmer.*

Short stories including "The Sea Bride," "Patchwork," "The Strange Companions," "Siren Song," "A Change of Aunts," "The Good-looking Boy," "The Whisperer," "A Fall of Snow," "QWERTYUIOP," "Masquerade." [Short stories]

7. Alcock, Vivien. **The Sylvia Game**. London: Fontana Lions, 1984. 157pp. ISBN 0-00-672138-9. (First published by Methuen, 1982). **A**

Emily Dodd's father, an impoverished artist, takes Emily with him when he goes to the country on "business." At first Emily is bored. Then while recuperating from the flu she meets Oliver and finds her life becoming more and more intriguing. Things become frightening, however, when Emily realizes that she is the center of a mysterious game, and all because she looks like dead Sylvia. [Ghosts]

8. Alcock, Vivien. **The Stonewalker**. New York: Laurel-Leaf, 1985. 151pp. ISBN 0-440-98198-0. (First published by Methuen Children's Books, 1981). **B**

Poppy Brown, unpopular because of her lying, comes to view a stone statue, Belladonna, as her friend. Then Belladonna comes to life and activates other statues as well. Soon Poppy is in danger, and she and her only human friend, Emma, must flee across the moors to escape the pursuing stonewalkers. [Magic; Transformation]

9. Alderman, Clifford Lindsey. **The Devil's Shadow: The Story of Witchcraft in Massachusetts**. New York: Archway, 1970. 182pp. ISBN 671-29299-4. (First published by Messner, 1967). **A**

A fictionalized account of what really happened so many years ago in Salem, Massachusetts. The frightened young girls who start the turmoil are confused, as is the rest of the small community, which reacts by destroying those people accused of witchcraft. [Witchcraft]

10. Alexander, Karl. **The Curse of the Vampire**. New York: Pinnacle, 1982. 310pp. ISBN 0-523-41874-4. **C**

A modern American movie actress on location in Transylvania becomes a victim of the vampire legend. Sinister, moldering Vladimir Castle becomes her refuge as she leads her double life of actress by day and bloodsucking vampire by night. [Vampires]

11. Alexis, Katina. **Scorpion**. New York: Leisure Books, 1986. 287pp. ISBN 0-8439-2400-4. **C**

Odd things are happening to Dr. Nan Bristow and her two beautiful daughters, one of whom is in a strange catatonic state. In the nearby woods a fearsome, ancient horror is being unleashed by ancient Cherokee rites and the final outcome is frightening and awesome. [Horror; Legends, Native American]

12. Allende, Isabel. **House of the Spirits**. New York: Bantam, 1986. 433pp. ISBN 0-553-25865-6. (First published by Knopf, 1985). **C**

The Trueba family of South America possesses wealth and mysterious powers. The various members of the family pursue different goals and dabble in mystic matters. They come to very different ends and find various degrees of happiness. [Mysticism; Spiritualism]

13. Amado, Jorge Luis. **Dona Flor and Her Two Husbands**. New York: Avon, 1969. 521pp. ISBN 0-380-01796-2. (First published in the United States by Knopf, 1969). **C**
     Movie Version: 1979 (Brazilian). Director: Bruno Barreto. Stars: Sonia Braga and Jose Wilker. American remake set in New York: *Kiss Me Goodbye*. 1982. Director: Robert Mulligan. Stars: Sally Field, James Caan, and Jeff Bridges.

Gentle, pretty Dona Flor was enchanted by her first husband, a charming, irresponsible rake. She mourned his death, but finally agreed to wed an upstanding, dull citizen of the town. To her surprise and horror, her first husband returns as a ghost to be part of her life and jeer at her new spouse. Dona Flor turns to voodoo to help her out of her predicament, but still cannot rid herself of her passionate love for her ghostly first husband. [Ghosts; Voodoo]

14. Ames, Mildred. **The Silver Link, the Silken Tie**. New York: Scholastic/Point, 1986. 254pp. ISBN 0-590-33537-X. (First published by Scribner, 1984). **A**
     Other works: *Anna to the Infinite Power*.

Tim and Felice are both haunted by tragedy from the past. When they meet, they discover a special ability to communicate on another level which helps soothe their emotional scars and bring new wonderment to their lives. [Paranormal abilities]

15. Anson, Jay. **666**. New York: Bantam, 1982. 280pp. ISBN 0-671-83126-7. (First published by Simon & Schuster, 1981). **C**
     Other works: *The Amityville Horror*.

The house has a terrible history of brutal murder. The Olsons are not happy when the house is moved to their neighborhood, but they little realize the horror which will soon start and change their lives forever. [Evil; Haunted houses]

16. Anstey, F. (pseud. of Thomas Anstey Guthrie). **Vice Versa**. Harmondsworth, England: Puffin, 1981. 302pp. ISBN 0-14-035067-5. (First published by John Murray, 1882). **A**

Young Dick Bultride is in trouble at school, but his father Paul believes this is all nonsense and that he'd love to be a carefree schoolboy again. Then, miraculously, a switch takes place — Dick becomes Paul and vice versa — with some hilarious results. [Transformation]

17. Armstrong, F. W. **The Changing**. New York: TOR, 1985. 244pp. ISBN 0-812-52754-2. **C**

A modern technological facility like Eastman Kodak shouldn't be subject to superstition and folklore. Yet something strange is happening to people in Kodak Park; they're being ripped to shreds by something bestial and inhuman. [Werewolves]

18. Armstrong, Sarah. **Blood Red Roses**. New York: Dell, 1982. 154pp. ISBN 0-440-90314-9. (Twilight series). **A**

Kate is delighted with her new mirror, an ornate antique that her rival, Tracy, also wants. Yet her pride in her new possession starts to diminish with the increasing sense of doom and fear which emanates from the mirror. [Evil; Possession]

19. Arnold, Margot. **Death of a Voodoo Doll**. New York: Playboy, 1982. 220pp. ISBN 0-867-21114-8. (First published by Jove, 1982). **C**

Amateur sleuths Penny Spring and Toby Glendower (an anthropologist and archaeologist) stumble upon a mysterious murder in exotic New Orleans during Mardi Gras. Voodoo rites and the mysteries of secret societies add excitement to this classically styled detective tale. [Cults; Voodoo]

20. Arnold, Margot. **Death on the Dragon's Tongue**. New York: Playboy, 1982. 224pp. ISBN 0-867-21150-4. (First published by Jove, 1982). **C**

Modern cults and ancient Celtic customs mingle in another Penny Spring and Toby Glendower mystery. This time the setting is the bleak coast of Brittany, populated with sinister cult members. [Cults; Legends, Celtic]

21. Arnold, Margot. **Marie**. New York: Pocket Books, 1979. 486pp. ISBN 0-671-81919-4. **C**

Marie Laveau was the most powerful voodoo queen of New Orleans, and her influence in this nineteenth-century city was incalculable. This fictionalized account of Marie's life provides a fascinating glimpse of her times and practices. [Voodoo]

Bachman, Richard. *See* King, Stephen.

22. Barber, Antonia. **The Ghosts**. New York: Archway, 1975. 244pp. ISBN 0-671-52763-0. (First published by Jonathan Cape, 1969). **A**

Can the course of history be changed? Two modern children have the chance to find out when two ghosts appeal to them for aid. Even though the terrible crime which killed the ghost children was a century ago, the ghosts believe that history can be changed if Lucy and her brother have the courage to help them. [Ghosts; Time travel]

23. Barker, Clive. **Volume One of Clive Barker's Books of Blood**. New York: Berkley, 1986. 210pp. ISBN 0-425-08389-6. (First published by Sphere, 1984). **C**
Sequels: *Volume Two of Clive Barker's Books of Blood; Volume Three of Clive Barker's Books of Blood; The Inhuman Condition; Volume Four of Clive Barker's Books of Blood; In the Flesh; Volume Five of Clive Barker's Books of Blood; The Life of Dark; Volume Six of Clive Barker's Books of Blood.*

Horrible and gruesome tales with a very original twist including "The Book of Blood," "The Midnight Meat Train," "The Yattering and Jack," "Pig Blood Blues," "Sex, Death and Sunshine," "In the Hills, the Cities." [Short stories]

24. Bauer, Stephen. **Steven Spielberg's Amazing Stories**. New York: Charterhouse, 1986. 234pp. ISBN 0-441-01906-4. **C**
Sequels: *Steven Spielberg's Amazing Stories, Volume II.*

Stories from the television series including "The Mission," "Vanessa in the Garden," "Guilt Trip," "Mr. Magic," "The Main Attraction," "Ghost Train," "The Sitter," "Santa '85," "One for the Road," "Hell Toupee," "No Day at the Beach." [Short stories]

25. Beagle, Peter S. **A Fine and Private Place**. New York: Del Rey, 1979. 256pp. ISBN 0-345-30081-5. (First published by Viking, 1960). **C**
Other works: *Lila the Werewolf; The Last Unicorn.*

A gentle, quiet man makes his home in a cemetery mausoleum and finds more romance in the world of the dead than he ever had in the world of the living. The only trouble is the ghostly lovers must fight for their existence in this semi-earthly astral plane in order to stay together. [Ghosts]

26. Bellairs, John. **The Curse of the Blue Figurine**. New York: Bantam/Skylark, 1984. 200pp. ISBN 0-553-15429-X. (First published by Dial, 1983). **B**
Sequels: *The Mummy, the Will and the Crypt; The Spell of the Sorcerer's Skull; The Revenge of the Wizard's Ghost; The Eyes of the Killer Robot.*

Johnny Dixon loves fascinating adventure stories about ancient Egypt and horrible curses. One day, with the discovery of an old blue figurine, he finds out that ancient curses aren't just stories but can be for real. [Evil; Legends, Egyptian]

27. Bellairs, John. **House with a Clock in Its Walls**. New York: Dell, 1974. 192pp. ISBN 0-440-43742-3. (First published by Dial, 1973). **B**
Sequels: *The Figure in the Shadows; The Letter, the Witch and the Ring.*

Only Lewis can save the world from the doomsday clock placed in his uncle's house by Isaac Izard, an evil warlock. Time, however, grows shorter and shorter and shorter as Lewis desperately looks for the solution to the puzzle. [Magic]

28. Bellairs, John. **The Treasure of Alpheus Winterborn**. New York: Bantam/Skylark, 1983. 180pp. ISBN 0-553-15419-2. (First published by Harcourt Brace Jovanovich, 1978). **B**
    Sequel: *The Dark Secret of Weatherend.*

Young Anthony is delighted when Miss Eells offers him a job at the library so he can earn some desperately needed money. He doesn't expect, however, that he will stumble into a strange mystery in the library, one which could cost him his life as he battles the powers of darkness. [Black magic; Evil]

29. Benary-Isbert, Margot. **The Wicked Enchantment**. New York: Ace, 1986. 149pp. ISBN 0-441-88669-8. (First published in the United States by Harcourt Brace Jovanovich, 1955). **B**

Anemone runs away from home with her dog because she hates her father's new housekeeper. Living with Aunt Gundala she learns of mysterious goings-on and resolves to solve the secret of the statue missing from the town's cathedral. [Evil]

30. Benét, Stephen Vincent. **The Devil and Daniel Webster and Other Stories**. New York: Archway, 1972. 128pp. ISBN 0-671-42889-6. (First published by The Countryman Press, 1937). **D**
    Movie version: 1941. Sometimes titled: *All That Money Can Buy.* Director: William Dieterle. Stars: Walter Huston, Edward Arnold, Jane Darwell, and Anne Shirley.

Any number of people have offered to sell their souls to the devil in times of desperation, but when it really happens, it will take the best lawyer in the country to get Farmer Jabez Stone out of the deal. In addition to the title story, the contents include "Johnny Pye and the Fool-Killer;" "By the Waters of Babylon." [The devil]

31. Benoit, Hendra. **Hendra's Book**. New York: Scholastic, 1985. 148pp. ISBN 0-580-33202-3. **A**
    Companions: *Max's Book* by Maxwell Hurley; *Sal's Book* by Sal Liquori.

Three dissimilar teens discover they have super powers. They form the Psi Patrol, a group forced to work together to learn about the wonders of their fantastic new skills. [Paranormal abilities]

32. Benson, Robert Hugh. **The Necromancers**. London: Sphere, 1974. 235pp. ISBN 0-7221-1615-2. (First published by Hutchinson, 1909). **C**
    Other works: *The Light Invisible; The Mirror of Shallott.*

When Laurie Baxter's love died, he felt as if his own life had become deadly and meaningless. Then he turns to necromancy to try to bring his beloved back, but finds that dabbling in mysterious arts has aroused more spirits than intended. [Black magic]

33. Berger, Terry, David Berger, and Karen Coshof. **The Haunted Doll-house**. New York: Workman, 1982. 92pp. ISBN 0-89480-206-2. **C**
Other works: *Black Fairy Tales.*

A photographic essay with spare text tells the mysterious tale of what happens on Sarah's thirteenth birthday. [Haunted houses; Transformation]

34. Berger, Thomas. **Arthur Rex: A Legendary Novel**. New York: Delta, 1978. 499pp. ISBN 0-385-28005-X. (First published by Delacorte, 1978). **C**

A contemporary view of the story of Camelot, with familiar figures fleshed out with modern problems. [Arthurian legends]

35. Bierce, Ambrose. **The Complete Short Stories of Ambrose Bierce**. Lincoln: University of Nebraska Press, 1970. 496pp. ISBN 0-8032-6071-7. **D**

Mysterious stories by a mysterious man who disappeared in 1916. Part I, "The World of Horror" includes "Haita the Shepherd," "The Secret of Macarger's Gulch," "The Eyes of the Panther," "The Stranger," "An Inhabitant of Carcosa," "The Applicant," "The Death of Halpin Frayser," "A Watcher by the Dead," "The Man and the Snake," "John Mortonson's Funeral," "Moxon's Master," "The Damned Thing," "The Realm of the Unreal," "A Fruitless Assignment," "A Vine on a House," "The Haunted Valley," "One of Twins," "Present at a Hanging," "A Wireless Message," "The Moonlit Road," "An Arrest," "A Jug of Sirup," "The Isle of Pines," "At Old Man Eckert's," "The Spook House," "The Middle Toe of the Right Foot," "The Thing at Nolan," "The Difficulty of Crossing a Field," "An Unfinished Race," "Charles Ashmore's Trail," "Staley Fleming's Hallucination," "The Night-doings at 'Deadman's'," "A Baby Tramp," "A Psychological Shipwreck," "A Cold Greeting," "Beyond the Wall," "John Bartine's Watch," "The Man out of the Nose," "An Adventure at Brownville," "The Suitable Surroundings," "The Boarded Window," "A Lady from Redhorse," "The Famous Gilson Bequest," "A Holy Terror," "A Diagnosis of Death." Part II (The World of War) includes stories, such as "An Occurrence at Owl Creek Bridge," which have supernatural overtones. Part III consists of tall tales in the American folklore tradition. [Short stories]

36. Bill, Alfred H. **The Wolf in the Garden**. New York: Centaur, 1972. ISBN 0-87818-008-7. 144pp. (First published by Longmans, 1931). **D**

A village in upstate New York about 200 years ago is the setting for this classic werewolf tale. After the arrival of the Comte de Saint Loup and his hound in the village, terrible things begin to happen which make the local citizens aware that the comte is not a normal human being. [Werewolves]

37. Birkin, Charles. **The Smell of Evil**. New York: Award Books, 1969. 187pp. (First published by Tandem, 1965). **C**
     Other works: *The Kiss of Death; Death Spawn; Devil's Spawn; My Name is Death; So Pale, So Cold, So Fair; Spawn of Satan; Where Terror Stalked; Dark Menace.*

A collection of short stories with horrific themes, mainly set in Europe following World War II. A pervasive mood of evil is present in these modern tales of the macabre, which are sure to send shivers down the reader's spine. Stories include "The Smell of Evil," "Text for Today," "The Godmothers' Green Fingers," "Ballet Negre," "The Lesson," " 'Is There Anybody There?' " "The Serum of Doctor White," " 'Dance, Little Lady'," "Little Boy Blue," "The Cornered Beast," "The Interloper," "The Cross." [Short stories]

38. Bischoff, David, Rich Brown, and Linda Richardson. **A Personal Demon**. New York: Signet, 1985. 253pp. ISBN 0-451-13814-7. **C**

Willis Baxter, college professor, sometimes drinks too much according to his colleagues. Willis has no choice but to agree with them after the night he conjures up a fetching female demon who will not go away the next morning. [Demons]

39. Bishop, Michael. **Ancient of Days**. New York: TOR, 1986. 409pp. ISBN 0-812-53197-3. **C**

When RuthClaire Loyd first spots the strange, primeval man in a pecan grove in Georgia, she doesn't realize he is more than a missing link from the past. His mysterious powers of communication seem to reach to the heavens, yet his own yearnings are for something much more attainable, a modern American woman. [Paranormal abilities]

40. Black, Campbell. **Raiders of the Lost Ark**. New York: Ballantine, 1981. 181pp. ISBN 0-345-29490-4. **C**
     Sequels: *Indiana Jones and the Temple of Doom* by R. L. Stine. Find Your Fate series books by different authors use the character of Indiana Jones (see appendix 1 for titles and authors).
     Movie version: 1981. Director: Steven Spielberg. Stars: Harrison Ford and Karen Allen.

A fast-paced story in exotic settings, focusing on the attempts of a dashing archaeologist, Indiana Jones, to thwart the Nazi plan to harness the occult powers of the ancient and mysterious Ark of the Covenant. [Legends, Jewish]

41. Blackwood, Algernon. **Best Ghost Stories of Algernon Blackwood**. New York: Dover, 1973. 396pp. ISBN 0-486-22977-7. **D**

A noted, respected author of Victorian ghost stories, and authority in supernatural writing, E. F. Bleiler, edited this collection, which includes "Accessory before the Fact," "Ancient Lights," "Ancient Sorceries," "The Empty House," "The Glamour of the Snow," "Keeping His Promise," "The Listener," "Max Hensig," "The Other Wing," "Secret Worship," "The Transfer," "The Wendigo," "The Willows." [Short stories]

42. Blatty, William Peter. **The Exorcist**. New York: Bantam, 1972. 416pp. ISBN 0-553-24569-7. (First published by Harper & Row, 1971). **C**
Sequel: *Legion.*
Movie version: 1973. Director: William Friedkin. Stars: Ellen Burstyn, Linda Blair, and Max von Sydow.

An actress on location in Washington, D.C. finds her daughter, eleven-year-old Regan, possessed by a horrible demon. Efforts to save Regan pit the frantic mother, two Catholic priests, and a dubious police detective against the evils and terror of Hell. The graphic descriptions and details of possession are not for the faint of heart. [Evil; Exorcism; Possession]

43. Blaylock, James P. **Homunculus**. New York: Ace, 1986. 247pp. ISBN 0-441-34258-2. **C**
Other works: *The Digging Leviathan.*

Grave robbers, mad scientists, and obsessed searchers into hidden secrets populate this funny story of Victorian London. [Black magic; Science gone wrong]

44. Blish, James. **Black Easter**. New York: Dell, 1968. 160pp. **C**
Sequel: *The Day after Judgment.*

A classic struggle between good and evil is portrayed. The cruel forces of the powers of Satan seem to be unstoppable, but one brave man is determined to succeed. If he fails, the consequences are unthinkable. [The devil; Evil]

Blixen, Karen. *See* Dinesen, Isak.

45. Bloch, Robert. **Bogey Men: Ten Tales**. New York: Pyramid, 1963. **C**
Other works: *Pleasant Dreams; The Skull of the Marquis de Sade and Other Stories; Strange Eons; Such Stuff as Screams Are Made Of; Cold Chills; Tales in a Jugular Vein; Ariel; Out of My Head.*

Famed horror writer and author of *Psycho* has produced many shivery tales of horror, including "The Animal Fair," "The Double Whammy," "Ego Trip," "Forever and Amen," "The Gods Are Not Mocked," "How Like a God," "In the Cards," "The Learning Maze," "The Model," "The Movie People," "The Oracle," "The Play's the Thing," "See How They Run," "Space-Barn." [Short stories]

46. Boothby, Guy. **Enter Dr. Nikola!** Hollywood, Calif.: Newcastle, 1975. 256pp. ISBN 0-87877-032-1. (First published as *A Bid for Fortune* by Lock & Bowden, 1895). **C**
Sequel: *Dr. Nikola! Returns.*
Other works: *Pharos, the Egyptian; The Lady of the Island.*

An exciting, international tale of intrigue, kidnapping, and supernatural activities. Will Nikola succeed in using the beautiful maiden for his nefarious purposes, or will he be foiled by Richard Hatteras? [Black magic]

47. Bradbury, Ray. **The Halloween Tree**. New York: Bantam, 1974. 160pp. ISBN 0-553-25823-0. (First published by Knopf, 1972). **B**
Other works: *Dinosaur Tales; October Country; The Martian Chronicles; The Illustrated Man; Dark Carnival.*

The true meaning of Halloween is discovered by some children who travel through time to find out about this most mystical holiday and to search for a missing friend. [Legends, Christian; Time travel]

48. Bradbury, Ray. **Something Wicked This Way Comes**. New York: Bantam, 1962. 215pp. ISBN 0-553-23620-2. (First published by Simon & Schuster, 1962). **C**
Movie version: 1983. Director: Jack Clayton. Stars: Jason Robards, Jr., Jonathan Pryce, Diane Ladd, and Pam Grier.

Will Halloway and Jim Nightshade are almost-fourteen-years-old in a small Midwestern town in the earlier days of this century. One night, about a week before Halloween, Cooger & Dark's Pandemonium Shadow Show comes to town full of fascinations and mysteries. When Will and Jim discover the secret of the carnival, they become fugitives from the sinister Mr. Dark. Can Will's father, the library's janitor, save the boys? [Black magic; Evil]

49. Bradley, Marion Zimmer. **The Mists of Avalon**. New York: Ballantine/ Del Rey, 1984. 892pp. ISBN 1-345-31452-2. London: Sphere, 1984. 1,009pp. ISBN 0-7221-1957-7. (First published by Knopf, 1982). **C**
Other works: *Night's Daughter.*

Morgan LeFay is the central character in this intriguing version of the Camelot story. [Arthurian legends]

50. Bradley, Marion Zimmer. **Web of Light**. New York: Pocket Books, 1984. 208pp. ISBN 0-671-44875-7. (First published by Starblaze Editions of Donning, 1983). **C**
Sequel: *Web of Darkness.*

Ancient Atlantis is a land of magic and wonder. Two sisters, Domaris and Deoris, choose different sides of a powerful conflict which will determine the fate of their world. [Atlantis; Lost worlds]

51. Bradshaw, Gillian. **In Winter's Shadow**. New York: Signet, 1983. 304pp. ISBN 0-451-12276-3. **C**
Other works: *Hawk of May; Kingdom of Summer.*

Guinevere tells her own version of the dramatic passion and the evil machinations that led to the end of Camelot. [Arthurian legends]

52. Brandner, Gary. **Cat People**. New York: Fawcett, 1982. 221pp. ISBN 0-449-14470-4. (Based on the story by DeWitt Bodeen). **C**

Movie versions: 1942. Director: Jacques Tourneur. Stars: Simone Simon, Kent Smith, Tom Conway, and Jack Holt. 1982. Director: Paul Schrader. Stars: Nastassia Kinski, Malcolm McDowell, and John Heard.

Beautiful Irena is haunted by strange visions and unnatural desires. Her yearnings do not seem to be like those of normal people, and she is fearful of finding out the truth about herself. It surely cannot be true that people become animals, or is it? [Manimals; Transformation]

53. Brandner, Gary. **The Howling**. New York: Fawcett, 1981. 223pp. ISBN 0-449-13155-6. **C**
Sequels: *The Howling II; The Howling III.*
Movie version: 1981. Director: Joe Dante. Stars: Dee Wallace, Patrick Macnee, and Dennis Dugan.

A tired young man and woman decide to go to the country for a vacation, but discover to their horror that their neighbors are a bit weird and the nearby woods are inhabited by strange beasts from which there seems to be no escape. [Horror; Transformation]

54. Brautigan, Richard. **The Hawkline Monster**. New York: Pocket Books, 1976. 188pp. ISBN 0-671-43786-0. (First published by Simon & Schuster, 1974). **C**

The old west hardly seems to be the place for gothic goings-on, but an old house in Oregon is the site of mysterious happenings and puzzling events. [Horror; Monsters]

55. Brennert, Alan. **Kindred Spirits**. New York: TOR, 1984. 320pp. ISBN 0-8125-8103-2. **A**

Michael and Ginny, two depressed teens, attempt suicide and fail. As they lie comatose, their spirits communicate, enabling them to understand their problems and learn to cope with life. [Paranormal abilities]

56. Bridges, Laurie. **The Ashton Horror**. New York: Bantam, 1984. 160pp. ISBN 0-553-25104-X. (Dark Forces series). **A**

Dennis, the new kid at Ashton High, joins a fantasy game club in order to make new friends. Little does he realize, though, that the game is for real and his lovely new girlfriend has been marked as a human sacrifice. [Evil; Fantasy games]

57. Bridges, Laurie, and Paul Alexander. **Devil Wind**. New York: Bantam, 1983. 152pp. ISBN 0-553-22834-X. (Dark Forces series). **A**

Peter doesn't realize that when he blows an old whistle he will summon a dreadful power from the ocean depths, one which he and his girl friend, Mary, must battle for their sanity and salvation. [Demons]

58. Bridges, Laurie, and Paul Alexander. **Magic Show**. New York: Bantam, 1983. 135pp. ISBN 0-553-22833-1. (Dark Forces series). **A**

What more could an aspiring high school magician ask for than an ancient book of secrets? What Chris doesn't realize, however, are the very real dangers as he delves deeper into the old sorcerer's book of dreadful spells. [Black magic; Legerdemain]

59. Bridges, Laurie, and Paul Alexander. **Swamp Witch**. New York: Bantam, 1983. 153pp. ISBN 0-553-23606-7. (Dark Forces series). **A**

It seems great at first when Linda goes to stay with her friend, Heather Clark, while her father is away. But the Clarks' servant, Tubelle, is a voodoo priestess who wants the best for her darling Heather, including Linda's boyfriend. [Voodoo]

60. Brown, George MacKay. **Time in a Red Coat**. Harmondsworth, England: Penguin, 1986. 249pp. ISBN 0-14-007401-5. (First published by Chatto & Windus, 1984). **A**

A girl is given two gifts at birth, an ivory flute and a bag of coins. The flute is magic, and through it she moves through time. As she progresses through many periods, she sees the horror of war and comes to be clothed in a red-stained coat, symbolic of the blood that has been spilled. [Evil; Time travel]

61. Brunn, Robert. **The Initiation**. New York: Dell, 1982. 154pp. ISBN 0-440-94047-8. (Twilight series). **A**

Most students in a new school think they're outsiders at first, but Adam realizes quickly that more is going on at Blair Prep than his casual first impression. Adam's invitation to join an exclusive club brings him face-to-face with a horrible secret. [Vampires]

62. Brust, Steven. **To Reign in Hell**. New York: Ace, 1985. 268pp. ISBN 0-441-81496-4. **C**

A tale from the very beginnings of time, in which the angels, led by God, battle with that clever devil, Satan, for supremacy of the universe. [The devil; Heaven; Hell]

63. Bryan, Amanda. **The Warning**. New York: Dell, 1985. 156pp. ISBN 0-440-99335-0. (Twilight series). **A**

Lois thinks it's great that Ronnie Reed wants her to be his girl friend and doesn't see through his selfishness. But her happiness is shaken when her typewriter starts writing her threatening messages. Who is sending Lois these messages? It isn't Ronnie, famous for his practical jokes. But who, or what, is it? [Prophecy]

64. Bulgakov, Mikhail. **The Master and Margarita**. New York: Signet, 1967. 384pp. ISBN 0-451-51701-6. (First published in the United States by Harper & Row, 1967). **C**

Russian communist doctrine does not admit to the existence of God and heaven, nor the devil and Hell. When the devil turns up in Russia with his entourage, things begin to happen that just cannot be permitted in a totalitarian state. [The devil]

65. Bunting, Eve. **The Ghost behind Me**. New York: Archway, 1984. 169pp. ISBN 0-671-49865-7. **A**
Other works: *The Haunting of Safekeep; Strange Things Happen in the Woods; Ghost of Summer.*

Cinnamon finds herself fearful of the lovely old house in San Francisco that is to be her summer home. Who is the elusive young man in the vintage car whom only she can see? [Ghosts]

66. Bunting, Eve. **The Ghosts of Departure Point**. New York: Scholastic/ Point, n.d. 113pp. ISBN 0-590-33116-7. (First published by Lippincott, 1982). **A**

Vicki, a vibrant seventeen-year-old cheerleader, finds herself living an odd existence after she is killed in a car crash on Departure Point. When she meets another ghost, handsome Ted, she realizes that she is meant to do something, but she cannot easily figure out what it is. [Ghosts]

67. Caidin, Martin. **The Messiah Stone**. New York: Baen, 1986. 407pp. ISBN 0-621-65562-0. **C**
Other works: *Cyborg; Aquarius Mission.*

Doug Stavers, a he-man mercenary, has a new mission – to locate the powerful Messiah stone, once worn by Christ and possessed of great power. Hitler owned it and nearly succeeded in his efforts. Now it is rumored that another man of evil is after the stone, and if Doug doesn't stop him, the world will be in trouble. [Legends, Christian]

68. Callahan, Jay. **Footprints of the Dead**. New York: Dell, 1983. 160pp. ISBN 0-440-92531-2. (Twilight series). **A**

Dani, shocked and stunned by her parents' deaths, returns to her childhood home in the Caribbean. She discovers not the peace she had hoped for, but rather horror in the world of zombies. [Voodoo; Zombies]

69. Cameron, Eleanor. **Beyond Silence**. New York: Laurel-Leaf, 1985. 208pp. ISBN 0-440-90582-6. (First published by Elsevier-Dutton, 1980). **A**
Other works: *The Court of the Stone Children.*

The recent death of his brother has troubled Andy greatly, but he becomes involved with an older, more ghostly tragedy when visiting his father's ancestral home in Scotland. At first Andy is only vaguely interested in this vacation, but as he learns more about the old Scottish castle, he finds himself drawn into an old, sad love story. [Ghosts]

70. Campbell, Ramsey. **Incarnate**. New York: TOR, 1985. 512pp. ISBN 0-8125-1650-8. (First published by Macmillan, 1983). **C**
Other works: *Demons by Daylight; The Doll Who Ate His Mother; The Height of the Scream; The Inhabitant of the Lake and Less Welcome Tenants, The Nameless; The Parasite; Hungry Moon.*

A frightening study of dreams, reality, and terror by a master of British horror. Centered around the aftermath of a scientific experiment on prophetic dreaming, the participants in the experiment find that their lives will never be the same again. [Altered states of consciousness; Dreams]

71.   Carey, M. V. **The Mystery of the Magic Circle**. New York: Random House, 1981. 143pp. ISBN 0-394-86427-1. (First published by Random House, 1978). (The Three Investigators series). **B**

Three bright teenagers get involved in a mystery of disappearing films. When they discover that the aging film star who takes the films is a witch, they find they may be in for more serious matters than they had bargained for. [Witchcraft]

72.   Carr, John Dickson. **The Burning Court**. New York: Award Books, 1969. 215pp. (First published by Harper & Row, 1932). **C**
      Other works: *The Devil in Velvet; The Demoniacs; The Dead Sleep Lightly; He Who Whispers; The Three Coffins.*

At first meeting, Marie Stevens seems to be an ordinary, albeit very beautiful, homemaker. She does seem to have odd quirks, however, such as a hysterical fear of fire. Could she possibly be a notorious nineteenth century murderess returned from the dead? [Evil; Ghosts]

73.   Carr, John Dickson. **Fire, Burn!** New York: Bantam, 1959. 214pp. (First published by Hamish Hamilton, 1956). **C**

When Detective-superintendent John Cheviot grabs a cab in 1950, he is delivered to the police offices in that same city, but in 1829. Due to his superior skills as a detective based on modern methods, he is able to solve a puzzling murder, but he also finds himself falling in love with a fascinating woman. [Time travel]

74.   Cassedy, Sylvia. **Behind the Attic Wall**. New York: Camelot, 1985. 315pp. ISBN 0-380-69843-9. (First published by Crowell, 1983). **B**

Cranky, disagreeable Maggie has been labelled nasty and disobedient, as well as difficult to manage. Maggie's great-aunts decide to take her into their big old house, and Maggie arrives prepared not to like it at all. After her arrival, however, Maggie begins to hear whispers that lure her into a magic world, one which changes her life forever. [Ghosts]

75.   Cave, Hugh B. **The Evil**. New York: Ace Charter, 1981. 309pp. ISBN 0-441-21850-4. **C**
      Other works: *Legion of the Dead; Murgunstrumm, and Others; The Nebulous Horror.*

Two idealistic Americans in Haiti discover the terror and mysteries of voodoo. Sam, an agricultural specialist, and Kay, a nurse, become embroiled in horror when Kay tries to protect a young Haitian boy, and Sam tries to help Mildred, a desperate heiress, locate her father in the steaming jungles. [Voodoo]

76. Cave, Hugh B. **Shades of Evil.** New York: Charter, 1982. 307pp. ISBN 0-441-75986-6. **C**

At first it seemed like an idyllic Florida retirement for Jack and Ruby. Then one morning Ruby sees a frightening figure rise up out of the lake, a figure which is bent on revenge. [Evil; Voodoo]

77. Chalker, Jack L. **The Messiah Choice.** New York: TOR, 1986. 380pp. ISBN 0-812-53290-2. (First published by Bluejay, 1985). **C**

Sir Robert McKenzie has turned his Caribbean island into a technological wonder, but when occult powers are invoked, the devil appears and injects midnight horror into the modern world. Gentle Angelique is aware of the menace, but her frail, paralyzed body may not be sufficiently strong to battle the ultimate powers of evil. [The devil; Evil; Science gone wrong]

78. Chant, Joy. **The High Kings.** New York: Bantam/Spectra, 1985. 250pp. ISBN 0-553-24306-3. (First published by Bantam, 1983). **C**
     Other works: *Red Moon and Black Mountain; The Gray Mane of Morning.*

Arthur was not the only glorious ruler in the ancient days of Celtic Britain. There were also Bladad the blemished prince, the two queens of Locrin, Leir and his daughters, and other legendary figures whose epic tales match those of the better known heroes and heroines of Camelot. [Arthurian legends; Legends, Celtic]

79. Chapman, Vera. **The King's Damosel.** New York: Avon, 1978. 143pp. ISBN 0-380-0196-7. (First published by Collins, 1976). **A**
     Sequels: *The Green Knight; King Arthur's Daughter.*

Lady Lynetta is destined to wed crude Gaharis, but she is rescued by King Arthur who makes her his royal messenger. Now her adventures really begin as she travels the magical and sometimes dangerous highways of the kingdom. [Arthurian legends]

80. Chayefsky, Paddy (pseud. of Sidney Aaron). **Altered States.** New York: Bantam, 1979. 205pp. ISBN 0-553-12472-2. (First published by Harper & Row, 1978). **C**
     Movie version: 1980. Director: Ken Russell. Stars: William Hurt and Blair Brown.

Eddie Jessings finds his in-depth experiments to discover his true self through hallucinatory drugs result in a dangerous near-loss of his innermost being. [Altered states of consciousness]

81. Cheetham, Ann. **Black Harvest.** London: Armada/Fontana, 1985. 143pp. ISBN 0-00-692199-X. **A**
     Sequels: *The Beggar's Curse; The Witch of Flagg.*

The Blakemans' family holiday in Ireland becomes more than they had bargained for when Colin becomes aware of an unnatural odor in the earth. Prill begins to dream of a death figure and little Alison falls prey to a mysterious illness. Only cousin Oliver stays calm, and it may be that Oliver knows more about the frightening events than the Blakemans realize. [Evil]

82. Christian, Catherine. **The Pendragon**. New York: Warner, 1978. 607pp. ISBN 0-446-32342-X. **C**

The story of Camelot as told by Bedivere, boyhood friend and faithful companion to the King throughout his eventful life. [Arthurian legends]

83. Clapp, Patricia. **Jane-Emily**. New York: Laurel-Leaf, 1973. 151pp. ISBN 0-440-94185-7. (First published by Lothrop, 1969). **A**
     Other works: *Witches' Children*.

In 1912, Louisa reluctantly goes to spend the summer with her niece, nine-year-old Jane, and her grandmother. Unhappy at leaving her boy friend behind, Louisa arrives at the gloomy old house in Lynn only to discover to her horror that Jane is battling for possession of her soul with Emily, Jane's aunt who has been dead for many years. [Ghosts; Possession]

Clemens, Samuel. *See* Twain, Mark.

84. Cody, C. S. **The Witching Night**. New York: Lancer, 1968. 286pp. (First published by World, 1952). **C**

The Indiana dunes serve as the locale for this story of modern witchcraft. Dr. Joe Loomis, vacationing in this peaceful local, starts to read his host's collection of strange books. Then he meets the fascinating Abbie, and his life begins to fall apart. [Witchcraft]

85. Cohen, Barbara. **Roses**. New York: Scholastic, 1985. 256pp. ISBN 0-590-33602-9. (First published by Lothrop, Lee and Shepard, 1984). **A**

A modernized version of Beauty and the Beast, in which Isabel must go to work for an ugly, deformed florist from whom her father has stolen a rose. At first Isabel is repulsed by her boss, and then she grows to like him, but she still cannot bring herself to kiss him when he asks. [Fairy tales]

86. Cohen, Daniel. **The Headless Roommate and Other Tales**. New York: Bantam, 1982. 138pp. ISBN 0-553-24628-3. (First published by Evans, 1980). **A**

Tales with a strong folklore element include "Introduction—Tales in the Night," "The Headless Roommate," "The Phantom Hitchhiker," "The Babysitter and the Telephone," "The Telltale Seaweed," "The Bordeaux Diligence," "Frat Man," "The Funny Collar," "The Moon in the Middle," "The Death Car," "Surprise!" "The Roommate's Death," "Gramma's Last Trip," "The Boyfriend's Death," "Just the Two of Us," "The Hook," "The Man in the Backseat," "Bugs, Ants, Baby Sneakers, and Spider Eggs," "The Joke," "The Moving Coffin." [Short stories]

87. Conaway, J. C. **Quarrel with the Moon**. New York: TOR, 1982. 319pp. ISBN 0-523-48033-4. **C**

Urban sophisticates, Josh Holman from the New York Institute of Anthropology and his friend, glamorous model Cresta Farraday, discover a colony which practices strange rites in the Appalachian Mountains of West Virginia. Can there really be werewolves roaming the hills? Terrible deaths and disappearances are happening, and there seems to be no possible, rational explanation. [Horror; Werewolves]

88. Condé, Nicholas. **The Legend**. New York: Signet, 1984. 399pp. ISBN 0-451-13266-1. **C**

An adventurous quest to seek gold becomes a nightmare when an ancient Indian god turns its wrath on those who dare to ferret out the secrets of Legend Mountain. [Legends, Native American; Shamanism]

89. Condé, Nicholas. **The Religion**. New York: Signet, 1982. 377pp. ISBN 0-451-12119-8. (First published by New American Library, 1982). **C**

A fascinating study of santería (modern voodoo) practices in urban America today. Anthropologist Cal Jamison is at first only academically interested in the cult's practices, but he discovers to his horror that his seven-year-old son, Chris, has been targeted as a sacrificial victim. [Voodoo]

90. Conford, Ellen. **And This Is Laura**. New York: Archway, 1977. 183pp. ISBN 0-671-55504-9. (First published by Little, Brown, 1976). **B**

Laura comes from a family of super achievers, and she thinks that even her good grades and successes aren't enough. Then she discovers her psychic powers which make her a real hit at school, but as her image of the future becomes sinister, Laura decides her "gift" may not be so wonderful after all. [Paranormal abilities]

91. Coontz, Otto. **The Night Walkers**. New York: Pocket Books, 1983. 164pp. ISBN 0-671-47523-1. (First published by Houghton Mifflin, 1982). **A**

Scary things are happening to the citizens of Covendale. Can one brave teenage girl save herself, or will she become one of *them*? [Evil; Science gone wrong]

92. Coontz, Otto. **Isle of the Shapeshifters**. New York: Bantam, 1985. 209pp. ISBN 0-553-24801-4. (First published by Houghton Mifflin, 1983). **A**

Is it possible for people to change into animals? Theo's visit to Nantucket brings discoveries about this legendary talent, as well as knowledge about her own ancestry. [Manimals; Transformation]

93. Cooper, Susan. **Over Sea, Under Stone**. Harmondsworth, England: Puffin, 1968. 221pp. ISBN 0-14-030362-2. (First published by Harcourt Brace, 1966). **B**
   Sequels: *The Dark Is Rising; Greenwitch; The Grey King; Silver on the Tree.*

When Simon, Jane, and Barney go to visit great-uncle Merry in Cornwall, they discover the magificent legend of King Arthur and the grail which is possessed of great power. Before their visit is over, they find themselves involved in a quest as important as any undertaken by King Arthur's knights. [Arthurian legends; Evil]

94. Corelli, Marie (pseud. of Mary Mills MacKay). **The Mighty Atom**. London: Sphere, 1975. 190pp. ISBN 0-7221-2544-5. (First published by Hutchinson, 1896). **C**
   Other works: *A Romance of Two Worlds; Ardath, the Story of a Dead Self; The Soul of Lilith; The Sorrows of Satan; Cameos; Ziska.*

An old-fashioned work which deals with the idea of purely intellectual, brilliant children who can be trained as superbeings. [Science gone wrong]

95. Coville, Bruce. **Amulet of Doom**. New York: Bantam, 1985. 156pp. ISBN 0-440-90110-7. (Twilight series). **A**

When Marilyn's adventuresome aunt dies mysteriously, only Marilyn seems to think that the old Egyptian amulet might have something to do with it. She knows for sure when the evil of the amulet turns on her, and Marilyn finds herself in a dark and dangerous situation. [Demons; Legends, Egyptian]

96. Coville, Bruce. **Eyes of the Tarot**. New York: Bantam, 1983. 152pp. ISBN 0-553-23895-7. (Dark Forces series). **A**

Surely the beautiful, strange deck of cards Bonnie finds tucked away in the McBurnie family attic couldn't be harmful. She becomes obsessed with the magical power of the cards and finds herself being sucked into a morass of evil, one from which she may not be able to escape. [Black magic]

97. Coville, Bruce. **Waiting Spirits**. New York: Bantam, 1984. 150pp. ISBN 0-553-26004-9. (Dark Forces series). **A**

Lisa and her kid sister Carrie are restless and bored on vacation until their grandmother shows them how to contact the spirit world by means of automatic writing. Suddenly, the game becomes serious business, and it looks as if the spirit world has come to be a dangerous and permanent part of Lisa's life. [Spiritualism]

98. Cowan, Dale. **Deadly Sleep**. New York: Dell, 1982. 167pp. ISBN 0-440-91961-4. (Twilight series). **A**

Jaynie had thought her trip to Scotland to stay with Evelyn and her family would be a pleasant change. Then the strange voices and shimmering glow from the nearby lake start to remind her constantly of the lake's tragic past, and perhaps of its frightening present. [Ghosts]

99. Coyne, John. **Hobgoblin**. New York: Berkley, 1985. 342pp. ISBN
     0-425-05380-6. (First published by Putnam's, 1981). **C**
     Other works: *The Legacy; The Searing; The Shroud.*

Scott Gardiner loves playing Hobgoblin in which he always takes the role
of Brian Boru. Scott, however, really believes in monsters, so it doesn't surprise him when he discovers monsters lurking in his high school corridors,
although he becomes very scared. [Fantasy games; Monsters]

100. Coyne, John. **The Piercing**. New York: Berkley, 1980. 261pp. ISBN
      0-425-04563-3. (First published by Putnam's, 1979). **C**

Betty Sue has become a national sensation with the weekly stigmata which
make her a controversy between those who see it as a miracle and those who
believe it to be a sham. Father Kinsella decides to investigate, but is he
motivated by religious belief or carnal lust? [Legends, Christian; Mysticism]

101. Crane, Caroline. **The Foretelling**. New York: Signet, 1982. 221pp.
      ISBN 0-451-12475-8. **C**
      Other works include books of suspense.

Psychics do not always welcome their gifts. Angela Dawn didn't want to
see the future when she looked into other people's hands. But it was worse
when she looked into her own palm and saw danger and terror traced in the
delicate lines. [Fortune-telling]

102. Crowley, Aleister. **Moonchild**. New York: Avon, 1971. 319pp. (First
      published in England, 1917). **A**

Beautiful Lisa becomes the student of an exciting man with amazing
powers who leads her into the hidden world of arcane knowledge. Then a
group of evil sorcerors decides to take control of Lisa, and her body and soul
become a battleground for occult powers beyond her control. [Evil; Magic]

103. Crume, Vic. **The Ghost that Came Alive**. New York: Scholastic, 1975.
      126pp. ISBN 0-590-09912-4. **B**
      Other works: *Mystery in Dracula's Castle.*

When the Blair family leaves on vacation, they little suspect that they will
be forced to seek shelter for the night in a gloomy old mansion. Mysterious
noises and goings-on complete the scene of terror. [Ghosts]

104. Cusick, Richie Tankersley. **Evil on the Bayou**. New York: Dell, 1984.
      148pp. ISBN 0-440-92431-6. (Twilight series). **A**

Young Meg has been volunteered by her mother to nurse an old aunt.
When her aunt recovers mysteriously, Meg knows her amateur skills are not
the reason, particularly when strange things begin to happen, including a
strange and sudden death. [Black magic]

105. Dahl, Roald. **Tales of the Unexpected**. Harmondsworth, England: Penguin, 1979. 282pp. ISBN 0-14-005131-7. (First published by Michael Joseph, 1979). **C**
     Other works: *Kiss, Kiss; Someone Like You; Charlie and the Chocolate Factory; James and the Giant Peach.*

Anthology of strange and macabre stories, some first published in other collections by the author, includes "Taste," "Lamb to the Slaughter," "Man from the South," "My Lady Love, My Dove," "Dip in the Pool," "Galloping Foxley," "Skin," "Neck," "Nunc Dimittis," "The Landlady," "William and Mary," "The Way up to Heaven," "Parson's Pleasure," "Mrs. Bixby and the Colonel's Coat," "Royal Jelly," "Edward the Conquerer." [Short stories]

106. Daniel, Colin. **Demon Tree**. New York: Dell, 1983. 153pp. ISBN 0-440-92097-3. (Twilight series). **A**

Maggie is the new girl in town, and she begins to think there are some very strange things going on in Wells. Even the fog seems oppressive and frightening. In the middle of Wells there is a big old oak tree that Maggie finds herself avoiding whenever she can, as well as the people, who are just plain peculiar. [Cults]

107. Daniels, Gail. **Cancer, the Moonchild**. New York: Pacer, 1985. 160pp. ISBN 0-448-47741-6. (Zodiac Club series). **A**

When Mara goes on a family vacation after breaking up with her boy friend, she isn't sure if she believes the Chinese fortune-teller who tells her that a new fellow will soon enter her life. Includes Chinese horoscope information. [Astrology]

108. Daniels, Gail. **The Stars Unite**. New York: Pacer/Berkley, 1984. 160pp. ISBN 0-399-21106-3. (Zodiac Club series). **A**

Abby becomes enthusiastic about astrology and persuades her friends to form an astrology club. Their new interest leads them into some interesting situations, not to mention some star-crossed relationships. Includes compatibility charts. [Astrology]

109. Daniels, Les. **The Black Castle**. New York: Ace, 1983. 240pp. ISBN 0-44-06515-5. (First published by Scribner's, 1978). **C**
     Sequels: *The Silver Skull; Citizen Vampire.*

Don Sebastian is a vampire, but his secret is guarded by his brother, a Grand Inquisitor, who provides his cursed brother with blood from the victims in his dungeons. [Vampires]

110. Daniels, Philip. **The Dracula Murders**. New York: Lorevan, 1986. 190pp. ISBN 0-931773-81-4. (First published by Robert Hale, 1983). **C**

It all starts with a Festival of Horror Ball, but before it is over there is a ritualistic murder and the shocking evidence that a vampire is loose on the golf course. [Vampires]

111. Darke, Majorie. **Messages: A Collection of Shivery Tales**. Harmonds-worth, England: Puffin, 1985. 140pp. ISBN 0-14-031749-X. (First published by Viking Kestrel, 1984). **A**

A collection of mysterious and scary stories which includes "Messages," "A New Way with Old Transport," "Truth, Dare or Promise?" "Christmas Spook," "Now You See Me, Now You Don't!" "Close Encounter of Another Kind," "Eggshell Saturday," "Peanut." [Ghosts; Short stories]

112. Davies, Robertson. **High Spirits: A Collection of Ghost Stories**. Harmondsworth, England: Penguin, 1982. 198pp. ISBN 0-14-00-6506-9. **C**

A collection of original ghost stories in the English Christmas ghost story tradition by a noted Canadian author and humorist, including "How the High Spirits Came About (A Chapter of Autobiography)," "Revelation from a Smoky Fire," "The Ghost Who Vanished by Degrees," "The Great Queen is Amused," "The Night of the Three Kings," "The Charlottetown Banquet," "When Satan Goes Home for Christmas," "Refuge of Insulted Saints," "Dickens Digested," "The Kiss of Khrushchev," "The Cat That Went to Trini-ty," "The Ugly Spectre of Sexism," "The Pit Whence Ye Are Digged," "The Perils of the Double Sign," "Conversations with the Little Table," "The King Enjoys His Own Again," "The Xerox in the Lost Room," "Einstein and the Little Lord," "Offer of Immortality." [Ghosts; Short stories]

113. DeFelitta, Frank. **Audrey Rose**. New York: Warner, 1975. 462pp. ISBN 0-446-36380-4. (First published by Putnam's, 1975). **C**
    Sequel: *For Love of Audrey Rose.*
    Other works: *The Entity.*
    Movie version: 1977. Director: Robert Wise. Stars: Marsha Mason, John Beck, and Anthony Hopkins.

Can Ivy Templeton really be Audrey Rose, a young girl who died in a tragic automobile accident? Her parents become more and more uncertain as strange events take place. [Reincarnation]

114. DeFelitta, Frank. **Golgotha Falls: An Assault on the Fourth Dimension**. New York: Pocket Books, 1984. 341pp. ISBN 0-671-50776-1. (First published by Simon & Schuster, 1984). **C**

An unhappy town has shut itself off from the world, but evil still seems to stalk its streets. Can the town be rid of its power? Will the combined power of one priest and two scientists be enough to overpower Satan himself? [Evil; Exorcism]

115. de Lint, Charles. **Moonheart**. New York: Ace, 1984. 485pp. ISBN 0-441-53721-9. **C**
    Other works: *Mulengro: A Romany Tale; The Riddle of the Wren.*

Sara Kendall loves old things such as antiques and legends. She is curious about fantasy and how it may touch the real world, but she is amazed when somehow she finds herself involved not only in ancient Celtic beliefs but in Canadian Indian lore as well. [Legends, Celtic; Legends, Native American]

116. de Lint, Charles. **Yarrow: An Autumn Tale**. New York: Ace, 1986. 244pp. ISBN 0-441-94000-5. **C**

Cat Midheir, a fantasy writer living in Ottawa, balances her world of reality and dreams very nicely—her dreams serve as inspiration for her stories. Then the Thief of Dreams steals Cat's dreams and she must go on a quest to get them back. [Dreams]

117. Dickens, Charles. **The Complete Ghost Stories of Charles Dickens**. New York: Washington Square, 1982. 408pp. ISBN 0-671-49752-9. **C**
Other works: *The Supernatural Short Stories of Charles Dickens*.
Movie version: *A Christmas Carol:* 1951. Director: Brian Desmond Hurst. Stars: Alistair Sim, Kathleen Harrison, Jack Warner, and Michael Horden.

Ghost stories by the famous English, Victorian author, including "Introduction by Peter Haining," "Captain Murderer's and the Devil's Bargain," "The Lawyer and the Ghost," "The Queer Chair," "The Ghosts of the Mail," "A Madman's Manuscript," "The Story of the Goblins Who Stole a Sexton," "Baron Koeldwethout's Apparition," "A Christmas Carol," "The Haunted Man and the Ghost's Bargain," "A Child's Dream of a Star," "Christmas Ghosts," "To Be Read at Dusk," "The Ghost Chamber," "The Haunted House," "Mr. Testator's Visitation," "The Trial for Murder," "The Signal-Man," "Four Ghost Stories," "The Portrait-Painter's Story," "Well-Authenticated Rappings." [Ghosts; Short stories]

118. Dickinson, Peter. **The Gift**. Harmondsworth, England: Puffin, 1975. 172pp. ISBN 0-14-030731-1. (First published by Victor Gollancz, 1973). **B**
Other works: *Annerton Pit*; and The Changes trilogy.

Davy Price is able to see what others are thinking, truly a gift. Davy is fearful of his gift, but finds he must use it to help his father. [Paranormal abilities]

119. Dickinson, Peter. **Healer**. Harmondsworth, England: Puffin, 1985. 214pp. ISBN 0-575-03314-2. (First published in the United States by Delacorte, 1985). **A**

Pinkie Blackfoot, a healer, has few friends other than Barry Evans, her protector. When Barry tries to free Pinkie from her stepfather, who is exploiting her talents for his own gains, he finds greater dangers than he anticipated. [Paranormal abilities]

120. Dickinson, Peter. **Tulku**. New York: Tempo, 1984. 216pp. ISBN 0-441-82630-X. (First published in the United States by Dutton, 1979). **A**

When young Theodore's father orders him to leave their besieged Chinese mission during the Boxer Rebellion, Theodore little suspects that he will end up in distant Tibet where magic and demons are real. [Legends, Tibetan; Mysticism]

121. Dicks, Terrance. **Cry Vampire!** London: Hippo, 1985. 105pp. ISBN 0-590-70405-2. (First published by Blackie and Son, 1981). **B**

Simon was always leery of the dark old house and when new tenants arrive from Transylvania, Simon is sure something is not quite right. Then animals start to suffer from loss of blood and Anna Markos disappears. Simon is sure vampires are to blame, but only his friend Sally believes him. [Vampires]

122. Dinesen, Isak (pseud. of Karen Blixen). **Last Tales**. New York: Vintage, 1975, 341pp. ISBN 0-394-7152-X. (First published by The Curtis Publishing Co., 1955). **C**
Other works include: *Winter's Tales; Seven Gothic Tales; Angelic Avengers.*

Mysterious, unworldly atmosphere haunts these stories by the master Danish writer. Includes "The Cardinal's First Tale," "The Cloak," "Night Walk," "Of Secret Thoughts and of Heaven," "Tales of Two Old Gentlemen," "The Cardinal's Third Tale," "The Blank Page," "The Caryatids," "An Unfinished Gothic Tale," "Echoes," "A Country Tale," "Copenhagen Season," "Converse at Night in Copenhagen." [Short stories]

123. Doyle, Arthur Conan. **The Best Supernatural Tales of Arthur Conan Doyle**. New York: Dover, 1979. 302pp. ISBN 0-486-23725-7. **C**

The creator of Sherlock Holmes was fascinated by the occult and wrote a number of short stories dealing with unusual happenings, including "The Bully of Brocas Court," "The Captain of the Polestar," "The Brown Hand," "The Leather Funnel," "Lot No. 249," "J. Habukukk Jephson's Statement," "The Great Keinplatz Experiment," "A Literary Mosaic," "Playing with Fire," "The Ring of Thoth," "The Los Amigos Fiasco," "The Silver Hatchet," "John Barrington Cowles," "Selecting a Ghost," "The American's Tale." [Short stories]

124. Drake, David. **From the Heart of Darkness**. New York: TOR, 1983. 320pp. ISBN 0-812-53607-X. **C**

Introduced by Karl Edward Wagner, these tales of horror by an experienced, respected short story writer include "Men Like Us," "Something Had to Be Done," "The Automatic Rifleman," "Than Curse the Darkness," "Firefight," "The Red Leer," "The Shortest Way," "Best of Luck," "Dragons' Teeth," "Out of Africa," "The Dancer in the Flames," "Smokie Joe," "Children of the Forest," "Blood Debt," "The Barrow Troll," "The Hunting Ground." [Short stories]

125. DuMaurier, Daphne. **Don't Look Now**. New York: Dell, 1985. 320pp. ISBN 0-440-12122-1. (First published in the United States by Doubleday, 1971). **C**
Other works: *Echoes from the Macabre: Selected Stories; Rebecca.*
Movie version: *Don't Look Now:* 1973. Director: Nicholas Roeg. Stars: Julie Christie and Donald Sutherland.

Stories dealing with possibilities of the supernatural in the lives of ordinary people include "Don't Look Now," "A Borderline Case," "The Breakthrough," "Not after Midnight," "The Way of the Cross." [Short stories]

126. Duncan, Lois. **Down a Dark Hall**. New York: Laurel-Leaf, 1983. 181pp. ISBN 0-440-91805-7. (First published by Little, Brown, 1974). **A** Other works: *Killing Mr. Griffin; Daughters of Eve; Locked in Time.*

At first Kit is unhappy at being sent to Blackwood, an exclusive school for girls, while her mother goes to Europe on a honeymoon. Then she decides the school will be okay when she meets the handsome piano teacher. She discovers, however, that her initial fears were not idle fancies, for there is a horrible evil at work in the school as the students develop strange new and obsessive talents. [Evil; Possession]

127. Duncan, Lois. **A Gift of Magic**. New York: Archway, 1972. 201pp. ISBN 0-671-60110-5. (First published by Little, Brown, 1971). **A**

Nancy has special powers—abilities that first frighten her. She learns to control them, but finds that she cannot always make them do what she wants. [Paranormal abilities]

128. Duncan, Lois. **Stranger with My Face**. New York: Laurel-Leaf, 1981. 235pp. ISBN 0-440-98356-8. (First published by Little, Brown, 1981). **A**

Laurie thinks her life is perfect as summer starts. Then she starts to have strange feelings, and she realizes that she is never alone. Who, or what, is the evil presence trying to take over Laurie's body, and maybe even her soul? [Possession]

129. Duncan, Lois. **Summer of Fear**. New York: Laurel-Leaf, 1977. 219pp. ISBN 0-440-98324-X. (First published by Little, Brown, 1976). **A**

Rachel's cousin, Julia, has just lost her parents and arrives to stay with Rachel's family. Everybody seems to like Julia, but Rachel senses that something is very wrong about her. Only Rachel seems able to recognize that Julia is unnatural, and only Rachel will be able to save herself from this frightening menace. [Witchcraft]

130. Duncan, Lois. **The Third Eye**. New York: Laurel-Leaf, 1985. 220pp. ISBN 0-440-98720-2. (First published by Little, Brown, 1984). **A**

In her senior year of high school, Karen discovers she has psychic powers which can be used to help the police find lost children. She finds, however, that her special power puts a damper on her love life until Karen discovers that romance doesn't always come with high school boys alone. [Paranormal abilities]

131. Dunlop, Eileen. **Robinsheugh**. New York: Ace, 1986. 201pp. ISBN 0-441-73201-1. (First published by Oxford, 1975). **A**

Elizabeth is furious at being shipped off to her aunt's while her parents visit America. She knows she'll hate Scotland and is miserable at the thought of the time she'll have to spend there. Then she discovers the silver mirror which somehow allows her to escape into time. At first it's fun to have a secret place to hide in, but then Elizabeth discovers that she can no longer control the mirror, for the mirror is controlling her. [Time travel]

132. Ellison, Harlan. **Strange Wine**. New York: Warner, 1979. 316pp. ISBN 0-446-30659-2. (First published by Harper & Row, 1978). **C**
Other works include science fiction novels.

Short stories include "What Killed the Dinosaurs?" "And You Don't Look So Terrific Yourself," "Croatoan," "Working with the Little People," "Killing Bernstein," "Mom," "In Fear of K," "Hitler Painted Roses," "The Wine Has Been Left Open Too Long and the Memory Has Gone Flat," "From A to Z in the Chocolate Alphabet," "Lonely Women Are the Vessels of Time," "Emissary From Hamelin," "The New York Review of Bird," "Seeing," "The Boulevard of Broken Dreams," "Strange Wine," "The Diagnosis of Dr. D'arqueangel." [Short stories]

Ensley, Evangeline. *See* Walton, Evangeline.

Etchison, Dennis. *See* Martin, Jack.

133. Eulo, Ken. **The Brownstone**. New York: Pocket Books, 1982. 322pp. ISBN 0-671-46090-0. **C**
Sequels: *The Bloodstone; Deathstone.*
Other works: *Nocturnal.*

Chandal lives in a lovely old New York City brownstone. Her life seems perfect as she surveys her beautiful home and handsome husband, but something strange is happening on the upscale upper east side, something that Chandal cannot control. [Evil]

134. Eulo, Ken. **The Ghost of Veronica Gray**. New York: Pocket Books, 1985. 279pp. ISBN 0-671-54303-2. **C**

Dorothy thinks she is the most ordinary sort of girl imaginable, so she is happy when she makes a new friend, exciting Veronica. During the gloomy rainy summer days Veronica introduces Dorothy to wonderful new ideas and finally shows her how to go into the past where she must do Veronica's bidding. [Ghosts]

135. Farris, John. **Son of the Endless Night**. New York: TOR, 1986. 503pp. ISBN 0-812-58266-7. **C**
Other works: *Wildwood; The Fury; All Heads Turn When the Hunt Goes By; Catacombs; Child of the Endless Night.*

A dark and terrible evil is loose in New England, an evil that is beyond the courts and the laws of humanity. Death and horror seem to be unstoppable. [Horror]

136. Farris, John. **The Uninvited**. New York: Dell, 1983. 272pp. ISBN 0-440-19712-0. (First published by Delacorte, 1982). **C**

Barry turns to mystical lovers after the death of her boy friend in an accident. Then her spiritual lovers soon take on powers of their own, and Barry finds her family, as well as herself, in danger as a result of her supernatural activities. [Black magic]

137. Finney, Charles G. **The Circus of Dr. Lao**. New York: Vintage, 1983. 119pp. ISBN 0-394-71617-5. (First published by Viking, 1935). **C**
Other works: *The Unholy City; The Magician out of Manchuria; The Ghosts of Manacle.*

One day a fabulous circus comes to a small, dusty Arizona town. The mysterious proprietor, Dr. Lao, seems able to perform any feat of magic, as well as introduce the townspeople to his exciting menagerie of mythical beasts and legendary figures from history. [Magic]

138. Forbes, Esther. **A Mirror for Witches**. Chicago: Academy Chicago, 1985. 214pp. ISBN 0-89733-154-0. (First published by Houghton Mifflin, 1928). **C**

A sympathetic portrayal of a seventeenth century witch, Doll Bilby, who prefers a demon lover to those of more mortal origins. [Witchcraft]

139. Foster, Alan Dean. **Clash of the Titans**. New York: Warner, 1981. 304pp. ISBN 0-446-93675-8. **C**
Movie version: 1981. Director: Desmond Davis. Stars: Laurence Olivier, Harry Hamlin, Judi Bowker, Burgess Meredith, Sian Phillips, Maggie Smith, Claire Bloom, and Ursula Andress.

Perseus, son of Zeus and Danae, is forced to become a plaything of the gods as he goes through life, first cursed and then protected by the whims of the Olympic beings. When he meets his true love, Andromeda, however, he resolves to let nothing stand in the way of her rescue from the dreaded Kraken and the mishapen Calibos — not even the famed Medusa with her head of snakes. [Legends, Classical]

140. Gardner, John. **Grendel**. New York: Ballantine, 1972. 140pp. ISBN 0-345-28865-3. (First published by Knopf, 1971). **C**
Other works: *Gilgamesh.*

The Beowolf legend as retold by the beast. How does it feel to be Grendel, the villain? In this version, Beowolf becomes the villain and is no longer the brave hero. [Monsters]

141. Garfield, Leon. **Mr. Corbett's Ghost & Other Stories**. Harmondsworth, England: Puffin, 1971. 139pp. ISBN 0-14-030510-6. (First published by Longmans, 1969). **B**

Supernatural stories by an English writer, including "Mr. Corbett's Ghost;" "Vaarlam and Tripp;" "The Simpleton." [Short stories]

142. Garner, Alan. **Elidor**. New York: Ballantine, 1981. 145pp. ISBN 0-345-29042-9. (First published by William Collins, 1965). **A**

The eerie strangeness of a bombed-out part of the city is an irresistible place to explore. Roland and his friends find more than shattered buildings, however; they discover the way to Elidor, a shadowy kingdom threatened by great evil. [Evil]

143.   Garner, Alan. **The Owl Service**. New York: Ballantine/Del Rey, 1981. 176pp. ISBN 0-345-29044-5. (First published by William Collins Sons, 1967). **A**

When Alison and Gwyn discover the beautiful dinner plates hidden in the attic they don't realize that they are going to be drawn into an ancient Celtic legend of tragedy and magic. [Legends, Celtic; Magic]

144.   Garner, Alan. **Red Shift**. New York: Ballantine/Del Rey, 1981. 156pp. ISBN 0-345-30071-8. (First published by William Collins Sons, 1973). **A**

The ancient stone ax is the key to time travel. Tom from the twentieth century finds himself living other lives, those of an ancient Celt in Roman Britain and a sober roundhead during England's Civil War. [Time travel]

145.   Garner, Alan. **The Weirdstone of Brisingame**. New York: Ballantine, 1978. 198pp. ISBN 0-345-29043-7. (First published by William Collins, 1960). **A**

Susan and Colin have heard about the powerful weirdstone and decide to look for it in the woods. There they enter a world of sorcery and danger, danger which may destroy them. [Fairies; Magic]

146.   Garton, Ray. **Darklings**. New York: Pinnacle, 1985. 309pp. ISBN 0-523-42368-3. **C**

A horrible evil is stalking a comfortable town and no one knows who the next victim will be. Those marked for destruction become crazed servants of the devil, who plays with their lives as though they are pawns on a chessboard. [The devil; Evil]

147.   Garton, Ray. **Seductions**. New York: TOR, 1984. 277pp. ISBN 0-523-43317-4. **C**

Tantalizing, seductive beings haunt the consciousness of bedeviled men. Once they succumb, the men lose more than virtue, for their very lives are sucked out of them by these evil demons of the night. [Horror; Monsters]

148.   Gilman, Charlotte Perkins. **The Yellow Wallpaper**. Old Westbury, N.Y.: The Feminist Press, 1973. 63pp. ISBN 0-912670-6. (First published by Small, Maynard, 1899). **D**

A frail and sickly woman becomes obsessed with the patterned wallpaper in her sickroom, with a climax of incredible horror. [Horror]

149.   Gilman, Dorothy. **Clairvoyant Countess**. New York: Fawcett/Crest, 1978. 224pp. ISBN 0-449-23561-0. (First published by Doubleday, 1975). **C**

A psychic Russian noblewoman investigates various crimes and finds solutions that frustrate the baffled police. [Paranormal abilities]

150. Gipe, George. **Back to the Future**. New York: Berkley, 1985. 248pp. ISBN 0-425-08205-9. **A**
Movie version: 1985. Director: Roger Zemeckis. Stars: Michael J. Fox, Christopher Lloyd, Lea Thompson, and Crispin Glover.

Marty McFly isn't a very good student and, like a lot of kids, he doesn't seem to care about getting ahead. But one day he is transported back in time where he meets his own parents as teenagers and realizes that his own future existence is in peril if history doesn't repeat itself. [Time travel]

151. Gipe, George. **Gremlins**. New York: Avon, 1984. 278pp. ISBN 0-380-86561-0. **A**
Movie version: 1982. Director: Joe Dante. Stars: Zach Galligan, Phoebe Cates, Hoyt Axton, and Polly Holliday.

A cute, harmless beastie generates a destructive, malicious pack of fellow creatures who turn a pleasant small town into a nightmare during the joyous season of Christmas. [Monsters]

152. Godfrey, Sarah. **Aries Rising**. New York: Pacer, 1984. 160pp. ISBN 0-399-21107-1. (Zodiac Club series). **A**

Abby, the founder of the Zodiac Club, is delighted to go on a bicycle trip with her science class. Much as she likes her Zodiac Club friends, she's ready for new adventures without her constant companions. Includes the names of famous people born under the different astrology signs. [Astrology]

153. Godwin, Parke. **Firelord**. New York: Bantam, 1982. 369pp. ISBN 0-553-25269-0. (First published by Doubleday, 1980). **C**
Sequels: *Beloved Exile; The Fire When It Comes.*

In this version of the King Arthur tales, Britain is a land still stamped with the Roman presence, but the beginnings of a new age can be seen throughout the land. [Arthurian legends]

154. Godwin, Parke. **The Last Rainbow**. New York: Bantam/Spectra, 1986. 424pp. ISBN 0-553-25686-6. (First published by Bantam/Spectra Trade, 1985). **C**

The old Celtic world of magic and druids meets the new age of Christianity in the person of an ardent young priest who will someday be known to history as St. Patrick. [Legends, Celtic; Legends, Christian]

155. Goldstein, Lisa. **Dream Years**. New York: Bantam/Spectra, 1986. 195pp. ISBN 0-553-25693-9. (First published by Bantam Hardcover Editions, 1985). **A**

Robert, a young drifting surrealist in the Paris of the 1920s, follows an intriguing young woman and finds himself caught up in the Paris riots of 1968. [Time travel]

156. Goldstein, Lisa. **The Red Magician**. New York: Pocket Books, 1983. 156pp. ISBN 0-671-41161-6. **A**

Young Kicsi has found life in her little Jewish village in prewar Poland peaceful. Then one day a magician arrives with terrible predictions about the Holocaust, but only Kicsi believes him. Yet there is little Kicsi can do, and fate rushes toward her, mixed with magic and fear. [Legends, Jewish; Magic]

157. Gordon, John. **The Ghost on the Hill**. Harmondsworth, England: Puffin Plus, 1982. 171pp. ISBN 0-14-03-1372-9. (First published by Kestrel, 1976). **A**

Jenny knows that Ralph, the sophisticated young university student who is new to her village, is greatly attracted to her, although she loves another. There are other attractions in the village as well, and a strange mystery of the past. Finally, a climax comes one summer evening which releases the ghost on the hill and resolves restive feelings. [Ghosts]

158. Gorey, Edward. **Amphigorey**. New York: Perigee, 1980. unpaged. ISBN 0-399-50433-8. (First published by Putnam's, 1972). **C**
    Other works: *Amphigorey Too; Amphigorey Also.*

Strange stories composed by a master of the understated macabre, with elegantly drawn illustrations, include "The Unstrung Harp," "The Listing Attic," "The Doubtful Guest," "The Object Lesson," "The Bug Book," "The Fatal Lozenge," "The Hapless Child," "The Curious Sofa," "The Willowdale Handcar," "The Gashly-crumb Tinnies," "The Insect God," "The West Wing," "The Wuggly Ump," "The Sinking Spell," "The Remembered Visit." [Short stories]

159. Goudge, Elizabeth. **The White Witch**. New York: Popular Library, 1958. 352pp. (First published in the United States by Coward-McCann, 1958). **C**
    Other works: *The Little White Horse.*

The beautiful gypsy girl, Froniga, fascinates people in Elizabethan England. Her talents are extraordinary, and frightening to some. She loves Robert, but will her exotic charms prevail over those of her rival, gentle Jenny? A fine love story with rich historical details. [Gypsy lore; Witchcraft]

160. Goulard, Ron. **Bloodstalk**. New York: Warner, 1975. 141pp. **C**
    Sequels: *On Alien Wings; Deadwalk; Blood Wedding; Deathgame; Snakegod.*

Vampirella, heroine of a comic book series, is doomed to stalk an alien world, Earth, in search of her necessary sustenance. [Vampires]

161. Grant, Charles L. **The Nestling**. New York: Pocket Books, 1982. 406pp. ISBN 0-671-41989-7. **C**
    Other works: *The Last Call of Mourning; The Pet.*

An old Indian prophecy has foretold the coming of an ancient predator to the isolated Wyoming valley. When it happens, the townspeople know they are in the control of something so powerful, so evil, that they will never be free again. [Legends, Native American]

162. Grant, Charles L. **The Hour of the Oxrun Dead**. New York: TOR, 1987. 284pp. ISBN 0-812-51862-4. (First published by Doubleday, 1977). **C**
Sequels: *The Sound of Midnight; Nightmare Seasons.*

Natalie, a librarian and widow of the town's chief of police, knows that something is very wrong in her once-peaceful little town. [Evil]

163. Grant, Charles L. **The Tea Party**. New York: Pocket Books, 1985. 312pp. ISBN 0-671-50511-X. **C**

Like many other quaint, old-fashioned villages, Deerfield has a big old house. Its name is Winterrest, but those who go there do not rest, nor do they indulge in genteel tea parties. Those who go to Winterrest find themselves in the clutches of an evil dwelling—a house that truly lives. [Horror]

164. Greeley, Andrew M. **The Magic Cup: An Irish Legend**. New York: Warner, 1985. 304pp. ISBN 0-446-32438-8. (First published by McGraw-Hill, 1979). **C**

Early Christianity vies with ancient pagan beliefs in this tale of ancient Ireland, and the love story of legendary King Cormac. Central to the story is the quest for that most magical and powerful of talismans, the holy grail. [Legends, Celtic; Legends, Christian]

165. Gresham, Stephen. **Dew Claws**. New York: Zebra, 1986. 335pp. ISBN 0-8217-1808-8. **C**

Johnny Ray is a troubled child, but his new home with caring foster parents seems to help erase the memories of a frightening background in Night Horse Swamp. Yet he cannot totally forget what happened there, nor will he be able to escape from the terror responsible. [Horror]

Guthrie, Thomas Anstey. *See* Anstey, F.

166. Hagan, Chet. **The Witching**. New York: Leisure Books, 1982. 331pp. ISBN 0-8439-2289-3. **C**

The Pennsylvania Dutch country is noted for its pastoral beauty and quaint customs. Not as well known as the tourist scenes are the ancient practices of some dwellers in this area, that of Pow-wow. Even that can be viewed as harmless and picturesque, but when people start to die, a greater evil is obviously at work. [Pow-wow]

167. Haggard, H. Rider. **She**. Harmondsworth, England: Penguin, 1982. 300pp. (First published by McKinlay, Stone, & MacKenzie, 1886). **C**
Sequels: *Ayesha: The Return of She; She and Allan; Wisdom's Daughter*. Also: *The Journey to the Flame* by Richard Monaco (see entry 291).
Movie versions: 1935. Directors: Irving Pichel and Lansing C. Holden. Stars: Helen Gahagan, Randolph Scott, and Helen Mack. 1965. Director: Robert Day. Stars: Ursula Andress, John Richardson, and Peter Cushing. (Later version, 1985, starring Sandahl Berger, was "inspired" by the book and is set in a futuristic world. It bears little resemblance to the original novel.)

Hidden deep in the mysterious heart of Africa there is a country ruled by a mythical white queen, She, who must be obeyed. Her reign has been talked of for centuries, for She is ageless and has lived for thousands of years. [Eternal life; Lost worlds]

168. Halkin, John. **Slime**. New York: Lorevan, 1984. 252pp. ISBN 0-931773-74-1. **C**

Most of us thought the worst terror in the sea was sharks, but that was before the deadly jellyfish menace appeared. Their slimy trail soon extends to land as well, as small jellyfish invade water pipes and sewer systems. Can the human race be saved? [Monsters]

169. Halkin, John. **Slither**. New York: Lorevan, 1980. 215pp. ISBN 0-931773-63-6. **C**

Most people don't particularly like worms, but then they don't fear them, either. But a new breed of worms is developing in the sewers of London, vicious, man-attacking worms who have an insatiable appetite for human flesh and blood. [Horror; Monsters]

170. Hallahan, William H. **Keeper of the Children**. New York: Avon, 1979. 189pp. ISBN 0-380-45203-0. (First published by Morrow, 1978). **A**

The story of a father's attempt to rescue his teenage daughter and her friends from a commune run by a Tibetan monk who has promised to teach them the secrets of the universe. [Cults; Mysticism]

171. Halliwell, Leslie. **The Ghost of Sherlock Holmes: Seventeen Supernatural Stories**. London: Panther, 1984. 254pp. ISBN 0-586-05995-4. **C**

Mysterious tales of supernatural doings, set mostly in England, include "The Late Mr. Llewellyn," "The Beckoning Clergyman," "House of the Future," "The Centurion's Road," "Blood Relation," "The Temple of Music and the Temple of Art," "Remembrance of Things Past," "Brain Scan," "The Blackamoor's Drum," "The Girl by the River," "Hands with Long Fingers," "The Viaduct," "Lady of the Midnight Sun," "The Moving Rocks," "Demon," "The House on the Cliff," "The Ghost of Sherlock Holmes." [Short stories]

172. Hamilton, Virginia. **Sweet Whispers, Brother Rush**. New York: Avon, 1983. 215pp. ISBN 0-380-65193-9. (First published by Philomel, 1982). **A**

Other works: *Justice and Her Brothers; Dustland; The Gathering.*

Fourteen-year-old Tree must care for her older, retarded brother. Through a ghost, Brother Rush, Tree learns about her family, her black heritage, and grows in personal understanding. [Ghosts; Time travel]

173. Harbinson, W. A. **Otherworld**. New York: Dell, 1985. 399pp. ISBN 0-440-16738-8. (First published by Corgi, 1984). **C**

The mysterious Amazon jungle sets the scene for this story of a youth, Alex Poulson, who is torn between the conflict of his exploitive father and the beauty of the simple life led by the Indians. Alex reaches out to the Indians who teach him the secrets of their mystical beliefs. [Legends, Primitive; Shamanism]

174. Harpur, Patrick. **The Serpent's Circle**. New York: Warner, 1986. 261pp. ISBN 0-446-30026-8. (First published by St. Martin's, 1985). **C**

The Little Brothers of the Apostles has long been a secretive, alternative monastic order with certain practices and rites not known by the outside world. The brothers of the order have long nursed a grudge against the Catholic Church which persecuted their pagan-based religion in past ages. At long last they plan to release their fury and power against their hated enemy. [Cults; Legends, Celtic]

175. Harris, Marilyn. **The Conjurers**. New York: Jove, 1985. 272pp. ISBN 0-515-08362-3. (First published by Random House, 1974). **C**

The presence of hippie youths in a small, peaceful English village results in conflict and strange occult happenings. [Cults]

176. Harris, Marilyn. **The Diviner**. New York: Jove, 1984. 312pp. ISBN 0-515-07877-8. (First published by Putnam's, 1983). **A**

Young Mark Simpson doesn't understand at first why he is drawn to the abandoned naval base. Through ghostly visions he finds out about the tragic history of the base and the roles played by his own parents in a frightening tragedy. [Ghosts]

177. Hautala, Rick. **Night Stone**. New York: Zebra, 1986. 592pp. ISBN 0-8217-1843-6. **C**

Little Beth doesn't like her family's new house in Maine. It's old, creepy, and full of shadows. Then Beth finds a strange, hand-carved doll which becomes her new friend, her confidant, and, finally, her master. Beth is soon to be an agent of evil. [Evil]

178. Hawthorne, Nathaniel. **Great Short Works of Hawthorne**. New York: Harper & Row, 1967. 372pp. ISBN 0-06-083074-3. (First published in various collections in the early nineteenth century). **D**

A collection of some of Hawthorne's short stories, which contain mysterious and supernatural elements, includes: "The Scarlet Letter," "My Kinsman, Major Molineux," "Roger Malvin's Burial," "Young Goodman Brown," "The Minister's Black Veil," "The Birthmark," "Rappaccini's Daughter," "Ethan Brand." [Short stories]

179. Haynes, Betsy. **The Power**. New York: Dell, 1982. 147pp. ISBN 0-440-97164-0. (Twilight series). **A**

One day Meredith finds an ominous package in her locker at school — a curl of what appears to be her own hair, with a message. It brings her deeper and deeper into the terrors of knowing and even possessing her innermost self. [Possession]

180. Haynes, James. **Voices in the Dark**. New York: Dell, 1982. 153pp. ISBN 0-440-99317-2. (Twilight series). **A**

Christie's dreams seem very real to her. She can't understand why after them she feels impelled to visit the barn night after night. She isn't really frightened of this strange urge, yet deep down she senses a powerful evil she cannot control. [Evil]

181. Hearn, Lafcadio. **The Selected Writings of Lafcadio Hearn**. New York: Citadel, 1979. 2nd ed. 566pp. **D**

An author with an exotic background writes mysterious tales with international settings, including "Kwaidan," "Some Chinese Ghosts," "Chita," "American Sketches," "Caribbean Sketches," "Japan." [Short stories]

182. Heinlein, Robert A. **Waldo and Magic, Inc.** New York: Signet, 1970. 192pp. ISBN 0-451-12365-4. (First published by Doubleday, 1940). **C**

A world and time in which magic is practiced as a commonplace craft is the setting for this charming tale of love and good versus evil. Archie Fraser is a hardheaded hardware and construction dealer. Not a magician himself, he avails himself of magical crafts. Then, demands for protection money and the evidence of demonic doings send him to Jemima and Dr. Worthington, practitioners for good. A classic battle between good and evil climaxes the tale. [Black magic; Demons]

183. Henstell, Diana. **Deadly Friend**. New York: Bantam, 1985. 323pp. ISBN 0-553-26380-3. (Published originally as *The Friend* by Bantam, 1985). **C**
Movie version: 1986. Director: Wes Craven. Stars: Matthew Laborteaux, Kristy Swanson, Michael Sharrett, and Anne Twomey.

Paul, a brilliant scientist, has never been able to relate well to people, but when he meets gentle Samantha he falls madly in love with her. When she is tragically taken from him, he resolves to keep her with him somehow, whatever the cost. [Science gone wrong]

184. Herbert, James. **Deadly Eyes**. New York: Signet, 1975. 205pp. ISBN 0-451-12246-1. (First published as *The Rats* by New American Library, 1974). **C**
Other works: *Lair; The Survivor; The Dark; The Fog; Domain.*
Movie version: 1983. Director: Robert Clouse. Stars: Sam Groom, Sara Botsford, and Scatman Crothers.

A story for those who love Lovecraft's "The Rats Behind the Wall." Human revulsion has long been centered on rats, and this book will provide additional fuel for this fear. Set in modern day London, which is under attack by huge rats who feed on live human flesh, the book includes many gross details. [Horror; Monsters]

185. Herbert, James. **Shrine**. New York: Signet, 1984. 458pp. ISBN 0-451-12724-2. **C**

Lovely young Alice can seemingly perform miracles, but a reporter, Fenn, is not so sure that her power comes from heavenly sources. Rather, it seems to reek of evil and doom, even as pilgrims mob the little village, seeking miraculous cures. [Evil; Possession]

186. Hilton, James. **Lost Horizon**. New York: Pocket Books, 1984. 275pp. ISBN 0-671-54148-X. (First published by Morrow, 1933). **C**
Movie version: 1937. Director: Frank Capra. Stars: Ronald Colman, Edward Everett Horton, and Jane Wyatt. 1973. Director: Charles Jarrott. Stars: Peter Finch, Liv Ullmann, Sally Kellerman, and George Kennedy.

Four escapees from a revolution find themselves in a mysterious land, site of the legendary Shangri-La. [Lost worlds; Mysticism]

187. Hindle, Lee J. **Dragon Fall**. New York: Avon/Flare, 1984. 139pp. ISBN 0-380-88468-2. **A**

Gabe Holden, a Canadian teenager, designs and constructs dragon/monsters for a small toy factory. Gabe views his creations with affection, until the night after a rock concert when they come to life and threaten Gabe and his family. The author wrote the book as a teen and won the first Avon/Flame Competition. [Horror; Monsters]

188. Hoffmann, E. T. A. **Tales of Hoffmann**. Harmondsworth, England: Penguin, 1982. 411pp. ISBN 0-14-044392-4. (First published separately in nineteenth century Germany). **D**

Grotesque and bizarre stories by an influential writer of the German Romantic movement. Sometimes there are rational explanations, sometimes not, for his stories, which include "Mademoiselle de Sudery," "The Sandman," "The Artushof," "Councillor Krespel," "The Entail," "Doge and Dogaressa," "The Miners at Falun," "The Choosing of the Bride." [Short stories]

189.   Holdstock, Robert. **The Emerald Forest**. Harmondsworth, England: Penguin, 1985. 252pp. ISBN 0-14-00-7775-8. **C**
Movie version: 1985. Director: John Borman. Stars: Charles Borman and Powers Boothe.

Little Tomme thinks the jungle is fascinating when he goes for a picnic with his parents. Then he is stolen by Indians who rear him in their traditions. Later Tomme discovers that he must make a difficult choice between the mystical traditions of his adopted people and the culture of the white man. [Legends, Primitive; Shamanism]

190.   Holdstock, Robert. **Mythago Wood**. New York: Berkley, 1986. 274pp. ISBN 0-425-08785-9. (First published by Arbor House, 1984). **C**

When Steven Huxley returns home after serving in World War II, he finds his brother working with their father in trying to make contact with mythic beings who live in Ryhope Wood. It soon becomes apparent that there is something very strange about the wood; perhaps it really is the home of another race of beings, one of them being a fascinating woman. [Legends, Celtic]

191.   Holzer, Hans. **Star of Destiny**. New York: Day, 1981. 192pp. ISBN 0-8128-7041-7. (First published by Stein and Day, 1974). **C**
Other works include many nonfiction books on the occult.

A fictionalized account of the magical and alchemical tests of Rudolf von Habsurg, Holy Roman Emperor in the sixteenth century. Although such experimentations were not unusual in his day, Rudolf finds that he might be in deeper waters than he realizes. [Alchemy; Magic]

192.   Hoppe, Joanne. **April Spell**. New York: Archway, 1982. 176pp. ISBN 0-671-46527-9. (First published by Warne, 1979). **A**

While researching a paper for school, Jenny Littleton attends services at a spiritualist church and meets a man who will have great influence on her and her mother. [Spiritualism]

193.   Horowitz, Anthony. **The Devil's Door-bell**. New York: Pacer, 1985. 159pp. ISBN 0-399-21140-3. (First published in the United States by Holt, 1983). **B**
Sequel: *Night of the Scorpion.*
Other works: *The Silver Citadel.*

Thirteen-year-old Martin is taken to live in a hostile new foster home after his parents are killed. Not only does his foster mother hint that he doesn't have long to live, he discovers a coven of witches in the neighborhood. [Witchcraft]

194.   Houston, David, and Len Wein. **Swamp Thing**. New York: TOR, 1982. 223pp. ISBN 0-523-48039-3. **A**
Movie version: 1982. Director: Wes Craven. Stars: Louis Jourdan, Adrienne Barbeau, and Ray Wise.

Born in a comic, resurrected in a movie and now in a novelization, this is a story of science run amok in the swamps. Dr. Alec Holland battles the forces of demonic evil, as well as trying to rescue his beloved Alice, but his body has been changed from that of a normal man to a half-vegetable creature. [Monsters; Transformation]

195. Houston, James A. **Spirit Wrestler**. New York: Avon, 1981. 288pp. ISBN 0-380-56911-6. (First published by Harcourt Brace Jovanovich, 1980). **A**

Young Shoona has been trained to be a shaman, a leader among his people. But he sometimes yearns for a more normal life, that of hunter, until he learns the meaning of his powers and the purpose of his life. [Legends, Eskimo; Shamanism]

196. Howe, Imogen. **Fatal Attraction**. New York: Dell, 1982. 170pp. ISBN 0-440-92496-0. (Twilight series). **A**

Mirella is the new girl at school, and Janet knows there's something wrong with her. It's not just jealousy over Mirella's beauty, and her attraction for Janet's boy friend, David. Mirella seems to have an aura of evil surrounding her. [Evil]

197. Howe, Imogen. **Vicious Circle**. New York: Dell, 1983. 147pp. ISBN 0-440-99318-0. (Twilight series). **A**

Jenny's life had seemed terrific until the children of Dorset started disappearing. Everyone is frightened now, and Jenny is especially fearful for her lovely little sister, Andrea. [Evil; Possession]

198. Huddy, Delia. **Time Piper**. New York: Tempo, 1984. 210pp. ISBN 0-441-81205-8. (First published by Greenwillow, 1979). **A**

When Luke goes to London to forget an odd young girl called Hare, he finds her there, along with some other children from an earlier age. Luke realizes, then, that his own scientific experiments are not the only way to travel through time, for the original Pied Piper has returned. [Time travel]

199. Hunt, E. Howard (pseud., David St. John). **The Coven**. New York: Fawcett, 1972. 159pp. ISBN 0-449-01989-0. (First published by Weybright & Talley, 1972). **C**
Other works: *The Sorcerors; Diabolus.*

Evil and witchcraft in Washington, D.C.? If anyone should know, it's the author, former Watergate conspirator and C.I.A. agent, E. Howard Hunt. Jonathan Gault, the book's dauntless hero, is summoned to investigate the murder of a mysterious singer whose routines were said to resemble tribal chants. [Voodoo; Witchcraft]

200. Hunter, Mollie. **The Haunted Mountain**. New York: Harper, 1973. 144pp. ISBN 0-06-440041-7. (First published in the United States by Harper & Row, 1972). **B**
Other works: *The Wicked One: A Story of Suspense; A Stranger Came Ashore; The Walking Stones; The Kelpie's Pearls; The Thirteenth Member.*

Natives of Scotland know and respect the sidhe (fairies). MacAllister refuses to give them the corner of wasteland they want, and the sidhe avenge themselves on the stubborn crofter by taking away his freedom. [Fairies; Monsters]

201. Hurley, Maxwell. **Max's Book**. New York: Scholastic, 1985. 151pp. ISBN 0-590-33203-1. (Psi Patrol series). **A**
Companions: *Hendra's Book* by Hendra Benoit; *Sal's Book* by Sal Liquori.

Max is a member of the Psi Patrol, the biggest member at six-foot-seven-inches. Like Sal and Hendra, Max can do all sorts of fantastic things. [Paranormal abilities]

202. Hutson, Shaun. **Slugs**. London: Star, 1982. 208pp. ISBN 0-352-31201-7. **C**
Other works: *Spawn; Erebus.*

A British "nasty," for readers who like their shivers in the repulsive vein. The slugs are coming, millions and millions of them, and they ooze along endlessly in their search for their favorite food, human flesh. [Horror; Monsters]

203. Ireland, Kenneth. **The Werewolf Mask**. London: Knight, 1985. 124pp. ISBN 0-340-35340-6. (First published by Hodder and Stoughton, 1983). **B**

Tales of terror for younger readers by an English writer include "The Werewolf Mask;" "The Haunted House;" "The Empty Tomb;" "The Girl Who Read Too Much;" "The Creak on the Stairs;" "The Eyes of Martin Franks;" "Deadly Creature;" "The Body Changer." [Short stories]

204. Irving, Washington. **Rip van Winkle or the Strange Men of the Mountains: The Legend of Sleepy Hollow or the Headless Horseman**. New York: Scholastic, 1975. 80pp. ISBN 0-590-40100-6. **D**

Two tales of strange happenings in the quiet mountains of upstate New York. One is about a ne'er-do-well who falls in with some very odd bowling companions, while the other is about a foolish schoolmaster who does not reckon on meeting the dreaded spectre without a head. [Ghosts]

205. Jackson, Shirley. **The Haunting of Hill House**. Harmondsworth, England: Penguin, 1984. 246pp. ISBN 0-1400-7108-3. (First published by Viking, 1959). **C**
Other works: *The Sundial; The Bird's Nest; The Road Through the Wall; We Have Always Lived in the Castle.*
Movie version: *The Haunting:* 1963. Director: Robert Wise. Stars: Julie Harris, Claire Bloom, Richard Johnson, and Russ Tamblyn.

Investigating a haunted house is never easy, but Dr. Montague takes on the task of Hill House with his assistant Theodora; Luke, who will someday own the house; and Eleanor, who is sensitive to poltergeists. During their stay, the house becomes more and more oppressive, and terror mounts as the investigators become terribly uncertain about what is going on. [Haunted houses]

206. James, Henry. **The Turn of the Screw**. New York: Signet, 1962. 452pp. ISBN 0-451-51669-9. (First published by William Heinemann, 1898). **D**
Movie version: *The Innocents:* 1961. Director: Jack Clayton. Stars: Deborah Kerr and Michael Redgrave.

The only possible salvation for two young children must come from their governess. Will she be able to protect them from the evil spirits that want them? Or is everything just the governess's imagination? [Ghosts]

207. James, M. R. **The Penguin Complete Ghost Stories of M. R. James**. Harmondsworth, England: Penguin, 1985. 362pp. ISBN 0-14-009017-7. (First published by Edward Arnold, 1931). **D**

Classic ghost tales by an English writer include "Ash-tree," "Canon Alberic's Scrapbook," "Casting the Runes," "Count Magnus," "Lost Hearts," "Martin's Close," "The Mezzotint," "Mr. Humphreys and His Inheritance," "Number 13," " 'Oh, Whistle, and I'll Come to You, My Lad'," "Rose Garden," "School Story," "Stalls of Barchester Cathedral," "Treasure of Abbot Thomas." [Short stories]

208. Jensen, Ruby Jean. **Best Friends**. New York: Zebra, 1985. 318pp. ISBN 0-8217-1691-3. **C**
Other works: *Home Sweet Home; Cat's Cradle.*

Little Barry is only three. Surely, he must be the epitome of childhood innocence. Yet, strange things are happening. Strange, and not very nice things. Can Barry's special friends, his pets, be responsible? [Evil]

209. Johnston, Mary. **The Witch**. New York: Popular Library, n.d. 256pp. (First published by Houghton Mifflin, 1914). **C**

Seventeenth-century England was the scene of great belief in and fear of witches. This is the story of an accused witch, Joan Heron, whose beauty could not save her from the terrified cries of a public who thought she had special, demonic powers. [Witchcraft]

210. Johnstone, William W. **The Devil's Kiss**. New York: Zebra, 1981. 449pp. ISBN 0-89083-717-1. **C**
Sequels: *The Devil's Heart; The Devil's Touch.*
Other works: *The Nursery.*

A terrible evil has come to the small town of Whitfield. Can it be that Satan has come to earth from his underground kingdom? [The devil]

211. Johnstone, William W. **Rockinghorse**. New York: Zebra, 1986. 428pp. ISBN 0-8217-1743-X. **C**

Little Jackie and Johnny thought the old rockinghorse was the most beautiful thing they had ever seen. But the rockinghorse, which can take them to strange and terrible places, is hardly a toy for good girls and boys. [Evil]

212. Johnstone, William W. **Sweet Dreams**. New York: Zebra, 1985. 397pp. ISBN 0-8217-1553-4. **C**

A mysterious light, some sort of satanic fire, flickers over the peaceful town. Then evil invades the very fiber and soul of the community of Good Hope, and only ten-year-old Heather sees what is happening. [Evil]

213. Kahn, James. **Poltergeist**. New York: Warner, 1982. 304pp. ISBN 0-446-30222-8. **C**
Sequel: *Poltergeist II.*
Movie version: 1982. Director: Tobe Hooper. Stars: Craig T. Nelson, JoBeth Williams, and Beatrice Straight.

Pretty little Heather seems to sense the presence of beings other than her normal family in the house. Soon it becomes clear that something is causing odd things to happen, at first only irritating and strange, then frightening. Finally, little Heather is taken away and her mother must find her in another world. [Demons; Evil]

214. Keene, Carolyn. **Nancy Drew Ghost Stories**. New York: Wanderer, 1983. 160pp. ISBN 0-671-46468-X. **B**
Sequels: *Nancy Drew Ghost Stories #2.*

Nancy Drew, girl detective, finds rational reasons for seemingly supernatural happenings. In spite of the promising titles, all the mysterious goings-on are discovered to be part of purely human schemes. Stories include "The Campus Ghost," "The Ghost Dogs of Whispering Oaks," "Blackbear's Skull," "The Ghost Jogger," "The Curse of the Frog," "The Greenhouse Ghost." [Short stories]

215. Kilgore, Kathleen. **The Ghost-maker**. New York: Avon/Flare, 1986. 162pp. ISBN 0-380-70057-3. (First published by Houghton Mifflin, 1983). **A**

Lee is part of a group of psychics in Cassadaga, Florida. He is not really a believer, however, until the seance when he finds his world of reality slipping away, and he no longer knows what to believe. [Paranormal abilities; Spiritualism]

216. Kilian, Crawford. **Lifter**. New York: Ace, 1986. 201pp. ISBN 0-441-48304-6. **A**

When teenager Rick Stevenson wakes up one morning, he finds he is suspended six inches above his bed. With practice, Rick perfects his special skills, only to discover that powerful men want to use him and his power for their own ends. [Paranormal abilities]

217. King, Stephen (pseud., Richard Bachman). **Carrie**. New York: Signet, 1975. 245pp. ISBN 0-451-13979-8. (First published by Doubleday, 1973). **C**
     Other works: *Salem's Lot; The Shining; The Stand; Skeleton Crew; The Dead Zone; Night Shift; Cycle of the Werewolf; Four by Bachman; Thinner; It*. With Peter Straub, *Talisman*.
     Movie version: 1976. Director: Brian de Palma. Stars: Sissy Spacek, Piper Laurie, William Katt, John Travolta, and Amy Irving.

A misfit teenager, awkward and shy Carrie becomes the butt of a cruel practical joke by her schoolmates. But they hadn't reckoned on Carrie's telekinetic powers, nor did they realize that Carrie wouldn't take their jeers quietly any more. [Paranormal abilities]

218. King, Stephen. **Christine**. New York: Signet, 1983. 503pp. ISBN 0-451-12838-9. (First published by Viking, 1983). **C**
     Movie version: 1983. Director: John Carpenter. Stars: Keith Gordon, John Stockwell, and Alexander Paul.

Teenage boys usually love cars, especially ones of their own. But Arnie's car, Christine, loves Arnie in return and will do anything to punish those who hurt her or Arnie. Christine is a jealous protectress, and her love for Arnie becomes all-consuming as she destroys Arnie's enemies, and then his friends. [Monsters]

219. King, Stephen. **Creepshow**. New York: Plume, 1982. unpaged. ISBN 0-452-25380-2. **A**
     Movie version: 1982. Director: George Romero. Stars: Hal Holbrook, Adrienne Barbeau, Leslie Nielsen, E. G. Marshall, Ted Danson, and Viveca Lindfors.

A comic book styled on the old E. C. Comics of the 1950s, with a series of short, gruesome tales told by a grim reaper figure. The stories have the sardonic humor King's fans adore, along with the violence and supernatural gore expected in this genre. [Horror; Monsters; Transformation; Zombies]

220. King, Stephen. **Fire-Starter**. New York: Signet, 1981. 401pp. ISBN 0-451-09964-8. (First published by Viking, 1980). **C**
     Movie version: 1984. Director: Mark Lester. Stars: David Keith, George C. Scott, Art Carney, and Drew Barrymore.

Charlie McGee has unusual powers; she can start fires just by thinking of them. Her strange gift is probably derived from the fact her parents took part in mind-drug tests long before she was born. Now government secret agents want Charlie, and they'll stop at nothing to get her. [Paranormal abilities]

221.   King, Stephen. **Pet Sematary**. New York: Signet, 1984. 411pp. ISBN 0-451-13237-8. (First published by Doubleday, 1983). **C**

At first it seems like a charming idea for a small Maine town to have a special place for children to bury their treasured dead pets. But then it becomes obvious that the real cemetery is not for pets and lies further back in the woods. People buried there can come back from the dead, but they are no longer human. [Legends, Native American; Zombies]

222.   King, Tabitha. **Small World**. New York: Signet, 1981. 311pp. ISBN 0-451-11408-6. (First published by Macmillan, 1981). **C**
Other works: *Caretakers, The Trap.*

Life in high places can do strange things to children, and Princess Dolly, whose father was once president of the United States, seems to be obsessed with her dollhouse. All it needs to make it perfect is a real live miniature person to live inside and make it a truly small world. [Transformation]

223.   Klaveness, Jan O'Donnell. **The Griffin Legacy**. New York: Laurel-Leaf, 1985. 184pp. ISBN 0-440-43165-4. (First published by Macmillan, 1983). **A**
Other works: *Ghost Island.*

A stay with her grandmother and great-aunt in the family's old ancestral home teaches Amy more than family history in the traditional way, for ghosts from the past seek her help in untangling an old mystery. [Ghosts]

224.   Klein, T. E. D. **The Ceremonies**. New York: Bantam, 1985. 576pp. ISBN 0-553-25055-8. **C**

A summer renting a quiet farm seems like a perfect way to do some research writing. The young college teacher finds more than he bargains for, however, in the seemingly peaceful countryside. An ancient ritual must be performed, and no one can stand in the way of the powerful evil which demands a human sacrifice. [Evil]

225.   Klein, T. E. D. **Dark Gods: Four Tales**. New York: Bantam, 1986. 261pp. ISBN 0-553-25801-X. (First published by Viking, 1985). **C**

Eerie tales in the H. P. Lovecraft tradition include "Children of the Kingdom;" "Petey;" "Black Man with a Horn;" "Nadelman's God." [Short stories]

226.   Knight, Harry Adam. **Slimer**. London: Star, 1983. 156pp. ISBN 0-352-31366-8. **C**

There are many mysteries about the sea, and in the sea itself. The horror of man-eating sharks is mild when compared to the disgusting and terrible slimer. [Horror; Monsters]

227.   Koltz, Tony. **Vampire Express**. New York: Bantam, 1984. 128pp. ISBN 0-553-24099-4. **B**

A game-style choice book in which the reader directs the action involving an expedition to prove the existence of vampires. [Vampires]

228. Konvitz, Jeffrey. **The Sentinel**. New York: Ballantine, 1976. 315pp.
ISBN 0-345-30437-3. (First published by Simon & Schuster, 1974). **C**
Other works: *The Guardian; Loch Ness: A Tale of the Beast.*
Movie version: 1977. Director: Michael Winner. Stars: Cristina Raines,
Ava Gardner, Chris Sarandon, and Burgess Meredith.

A dedicated sentinel must guard the gateway to hell in order to protect the
world from evil, and the gateway is in Brooklyn. New sentinels must be
selected at times for this awesome duty, and there is no escaping the charge,
once a choice has been made. [Evil; Hell]

229. Koontz, Dean. (See also Richard Paige, pseud.). **Darkfall**. New York:
Berkley, 1984. 371pp. ISBN 0-425-07187-1. (First published by W. M.
Allen, 1984). **C**
Other works: *Whispers; Night Chills; Dreams; The Face of Fear;
Shattered; The Vision.*

Terrible ratlike things are attacking people. At first people thought they
were rats, but then it became increasingly clear that the attackers were worse
than rats could possibly be. [Horror; Monsters]

230. Koontz, Dean. **Phantoms**. New York: Berkley, 1983. 425pp. ISBN
0-425-06568-5. (First published by Putnam's, 1983). **C**

Jenny Paige, a young doctor, arrives in lovely Snowfield with her kid
sister. However, instead of the wonderful new life she had expected, she finds
death and unspeakable horror. [Horror]

231. Kotzwinkle, William. **Fata Morgana**. New York: Avon/Bard, 1983.
195pp. ISBN 0-380-64691-9. (First published by Knopf, 1977). **C**
Other works: *Doctor Rat; Elephant Bangs Tree; The Fan Man;
Nightbook; Swimmer in the Secret Sea.*

Police Inspector Paul Picard finds himself in a bewildering and mystical
subworld of magic and legerdemain as he investigates a murder in nineteenth
century Europe. [Legerdemain; Magic]

232. Kroll, Joanna. **Sagittarius Serving**. New York: Bantam, 1985. 160pp.
ISBN 0-399-21188-8. (Zodiac Club series). **A**

Penny, a competitive tennis player, learns that winning isn't
everything—in order to have friends she must learn to be sensitive to others'
needs. Includes sports for each zodiac sign. [Astrology]

233. Kurtz, Katherine. **Lammas Night**. New York: Ballantine, 1983. 438pp.
ISBN 0-345-29516-1. **C**

The witches of England are rumored to have called up the storms
that destroyed the Spanish Armada many years ago. Can contemporary
witches stop the Nazi horror from invading England during World War II?
[Witchcraft]

234. Lagerkvist, Par. **The Sibyl**. New York: Vintage, 1963. 154pp. ISBN 0-394-70240-9. (First published as *Sibyllan* by Bonnier in Sweden, 1956. First English version published by Chatto and Windus, 1958). **C**

The story of a priestess of the oracle of Delphi whose devotion to the pagan gods leads to heartbreak. A parable comparing pagan and Christian philosophies. [Mysticism]

235. Laski, Marghanita. **The Victorian Chaise Longue**. Chicago: Academy Chicago, 1984. 119pp. ISBN 0-89733-097-8. (First published by Houghton Mifflin, 1953). **C**

Attractive Melanie Langdon is ill, although not desperately so. When she falls asleep in her lovely old Victorian chaise longue she awakens to a world very different from the one she knows. She has gone back in time, and there appears to be no way to get back to her beloved husband and child. [Time travel]

236. Laubenthal, Sanders Anne. **Excalibur**. New York: Ballantine, 1973. 236pp. ISBN 0-345-23416-2. **C**

The Holy Grail and Excalibur on the Gulf Coast of the United States? Is it possible? Yes, if the legendary Madoc brought them in his twelfth century voyage to the New World. [Arthurian legends]

237. Lawrence, Louise. **The Earth Witch**. New York: Ace, 1986. 183pp. ISBN 0-441-18130-9. (First published by Harper & Row, 1981). **A**

At first Owen is attracted to Bronwen through pity, but as she grows more beautiful each day with the ripening of the summer crops, his pity turns to love and passion. Yet it would seem that their love cannot be, for Bronwen is not human. [Legends, Celtic]

238. Lawrence, S. J. **Aquarius Ahoy!** New York: Pacer, 1985. 160pp. ISBN 0-399-21222-1. (Zodiac Club series). **A**

The Zodiac Club members are staunch friends for the most part, but when J. L., Jessica, and Penny all decide they like the same guy, the stars begin to clash. Includes best vacation locations for different signs of the zodiac. [Astrology]

239. Laws, Stephen. **Ghosttrain**. New York: TOR, 1986. 314pp. ISBN 0-812-52100-5. (First published by Beaufort, 1985). **C**

Mark Davies had fallen from a rushing train, and now every day is a waking hell of fear. Something is driving him back to the train station and the horrible train of terror, and Mark must get on to the ghosttrain once again. [Horror]

240. Laymon, Carl. **Nightmare Lake**. New York: Dell, 1983. 146pp. ISBN 0-440-95945-4. (Twilight series). **A**

An idyllic summer vacation with their family shouldn't have frightened Burt and his sister, Sammi. After they discover a skeleton and later another body, however, they know their vacation is not going to be peaceful and restful. [Evil; Horror]

241. Lee, Tanith. **Lycanthia: Or, the Children of Wolves**. New York: NAL/DAW, 1981. 220pp. ISBN 0-87997-610-1. **C**
Other works include: *Sabella: Or the Blood Stone; The Gorgon—and Other Beastly Tales; The Winter Players; Companions on the Road; Volkhavaar; East of Midnight.*

Christian Dorse finds that he is not the only claimant to his ancestral mansion; two werewolves also declare their rights. [Exorcism; Werewolves]

242. Lee, Tanith. **Red as Blood: Or, Tales from the Sisters Grimmer**. New York: Daw, 1983. 208pp. ISBN 0-87997-790-6. **C**

Macabre reworkings of familiar fairy tale themes include "Paid Piper," "Red as Blood," "Thorns," "When the Clock Strikes," "The Golden Rope," "The Princess and Her Future," "Wolfland," "Black as Ink," "Beauty." [Fairy tales; Short stories]

243. Le Fanu, J. Sheridan. **Best Ghost Stories**. New York: Dover, 1975. 467pp. ISBN 0-486-20415-4. **D**
Movie versions of "Carmilla": *Blood and Roses:* 1961. Director: Roger Vadim. Stars: Mel Ferrer, Elsa Martinelli, and Annette Vadim. *The Vampire Lovers:* 1971. Director: Roy Baker. Stars: Ingrid Pitt, Pippa Steele, and Madeleine Smith.

Eerie works by a much admired and imitated early gothic writer. This collection, which is edited by E. F. Bleiler, a respected scholar in the field, includes "The Vampire Lovers," "An Account of Some Strange Disturbances in Aungier Street," "An Authentic Narrative of a Haunted House," "The Dead Sexton," "The Familiar," "The Fortunes of Sir Robert Ardagh," "Ghost Stories of the Tiled House," "Green Tea," "The Haunted Baronet," "Madain Crowl's Ghost," "Mr. Justice Harbottle," "Schalken the Painter," "Sir Dominick's Bargain," "Squire Toby's Will," "Ultor de Lacy," "The White Cat of Drumgunniol." [Ghosts; Short stories]

244. Leiber, Fritz. **Conjure Wife**. New York: Ace, 1984. 224pp. ISBN 0-441-11749-X. New York: Award Books, 1968. 188pp. (First published by Twayne, 1953). **C**
Other works: *Gather, Darkness!; Night's Black Agents; Two Sought Adventure; Shadows with Eyes; Heroes and Horrors: Night Monsters; The Secret Songs; The Sinful Ones.*
Movie versions: *Weird Woman:* 1944. Director: Reginald LeBorg. Stars: Lon Chaney, Jr., Anne Gwynne, and Evelyn Ankers. *Burn, Witch, Burn:* 1962. Director: Sidney Hayers. Stars: Janet Blair, Peter Wyngarde, and Margaret Johnston. *Witches' Brew:* 1980. Director: Richard Schorr. Stars: Lana Turner, Richard Benjamin, and Teri Garr.

Sociology professor Norman Saylor is horrified to discover that his wife, Tansy, is dabbling in witchcraft. She assures him that she is using her skills only to protect them from the evil doings of others at Hempnell College, but Norman insists that she destroy her wares and give up occult arts. After she does, terrible things begin to happen, proving that Tansy was right. When Tansy's very soul is captured, Norman realizes he must fight witchcraft on its own ground. [Black magic; Voodoo]

245. Leiber, Fritz. **Our Lady of Darkness**. New York: Ace, 1984. 183pp. ISBN 0-441-64417-1. (First published by Berkley-Putnam, 1977). **C**

Franz Westen's life has become disoriented and meaningless since the death of his wife. Then he realizes that the solitude he yearns for is haunted by chilling presences — paramental entities. The fragile relationships he has allowed into his life now become his bastion against evil. [Evil]

246. Leroux, Gaston. **The Phantom of the Opera**. New York: Carroll & Graf, 1986. 357pp. ISBN 0-88184-249-4. (First published in France, 1912). **D**
       Movie versions: 1925. Director: Rupert Julian. Stars: Lon Chaney, Mary Philbin, and Norman Kerry. 1943. Director: Arthur Lubin. Stars: Claude Rains, Susannah Foster, and Nelson Eddy. 1962. Director: Terence Fisher. Stars: Herbert Lom, Heather Sears, and Thorley Walters. 1983. Director: Robert Markowitz. Stars: Maximillian Schell, Jane Seymour, and Michael York.

The huge and imposing Opera House in Paris has many secret nooks and crannies. Lovely young Christine is anxious about her career and accepts the instruction of a mysterious hooded man who appears out of nowhere in order to help her. Little does she suspect, however, that the man is nursing a terrible grudge, as well as great love for her. [Horror]

247. Leven, Jeremy. **Satan: His Psychotherapy and Cure by the Unfortunate Dr. Kassler, J.S.P.S.** New York: Ballantine, 1983. 512pp. ISBN 0-345-30265-6. (First published by Knopf, 1982). **C**

Satan returns to earth in the form of a computer and seeks the aid of a psychotherapist. His chosen therapist, Dr. Kassler, finds his new patient to be very different from his usual clients, with some very funny results. [The devil]

248. Levin, Ira. **Rosemary's Baby**. New York: Dell, 1985. 218pp. ISBN 0-440-17541-0. (First published by Random House, 1967). **C**
       Other works: *Boys From Brazil; The Stepford Wives.*
       Movie version: 1968. Director: Roman Polanski. Stars: Mia Farrow, John Cassavetes, Ray Milland, and Ruth Gordon.

Pretty Rosemary, married to a struggling young actor, wants to have a baby, but her husband, Guy, wants to wait until his career is better established. Then they move to the apartment of their dreams and things start to happen. Guy's career takes off and Rosemary becomes pregnant. Other things, however, make Rosemary think that all is not well, and her fears for her unborn baby become paramount. [The devil; Satanism]

249. Lindsay, Joan. **Picnic at Hanging Rock**. Harmondsworth, England: Penguin, 1970. 213pp. ISBN 0-1400-3119-9. (First published by Cheshire, 1967). **A**
       Movie version: 1975. Director: Peter Weir. Stars: Rachel Roberts, Dominic Guard, and Helen Morse.

A picnic at Hanging Rock on Valentine Day, 1900, seems like a festive idea for the Australian schoolgirls who set off for their outing in high spirits. Those who return, however, are badly frightened, and some never come back at all. What could have happened at that mysterious rocky site? [Disappearances]

250. Liquori, Sal. **Sal's Book**. New York: Scholastic, 1985. 148pp. ISBN 0-590-33201-5. (Psi Patrol series). **A**
Companions: *Max's Book* by Maxwell Hurley; *Hendra's Book* by Hendra Benoit.

Sal likes being cool. However, his newly acquired psychic powers make him a member of the Psi Patrol along with two other teens he considers real creeps. [Paranormal abilities]

251. Lively, Penelope. **Astercote**. London: Pan Books, 1973. 159pp. ISBN 0-330-23672-5. (First published by William Heinemann, 1970). **A**
Other works: *The Whispering Knights; The Driftaway; Going Back; The Voyage of QV 66.*

When Peter and Mair first encounter Astercote, they cannot see it at all. Then they are told that Astercote, a deserted village, is all around them. The puzzlement grows as they learn more about the village and its mysterious past. [Magic]

252. Lively, Penelope. **The Ghost of Thomas Kempe**. Harmondsworth, England: Puffin, 1984. 159pp. ISBN 0-14-031496-2. (First published by William Heinemann, 1973). **B**

Young James thinks the family's new house is great, mostly because it's so old. Yet it isn't until later that he realizes the house is old enough to have a resident ghost, a sorcerer who causes all kinds of problems. [Ghosts; Haunted houses]

253. Lively, Penelope. **The House in Norham Gardens**. Harmondsworth, England: Puffin, 1986. 174pp. ISBN 0-14-031976-X. (First published by William Heinemann, 1974). **B**

Fourteen-year-old Clare lives in a wonderful old house in Oxford stuffed full of anthropological treasures discovered years ago by her great-grandfather. One item, though, a shield from New Guinea, seems to have special powers, and Clare finds herself having strange and haunting dreams of another place far away. [Altered states of consciousness; Legends, Oceanic]

254. Lively, Penelope. **The Wild Hunt of the Ghost Hounds**. New York: Ace, 1986. 150pp. ISBN 0-441-88810-0. (First published by William Heinemann, 1971). **A**

When thirteen-year-old Lucy arrives to spend her summer holiday with her aunt, she hopes to renew some old friendships. Everyone is growing up and changing, however. Caroline and Louise seem interested only in their ponies, and Kester has become a loner. Then the villagers revive an ancient hunting dance, and Kester's uncle predicts dire happenings. [Legends, Celtic]

255. Llewelyn, Morgan. **The Horse Goddess**. New York: Pocket Books, 1983. 464pp. ISBN 0-671-46055-2. (First published by Houghton Mifflin, 1982). **C**

Epona, daughter of a Celtic chieftan in ancient Europe, is so anxious to flee the responsibilities and life of a shaman that she runs away from her village with a Scythian stranger. She becomes his woman and learns to love his way of life on the Sea of Grass, but she finds she cannot escape her destiny and her special powers. [Legends, Celtic; Shamanism]

256. Logan, Les. **The Game**. New York: Bantam, 1983. 149pp. ISBN 0-553-22835-8. (Dark Forces series). **A**

Ouija becomes the means for a demon to take over crippled Julie and, consequently, her attempts to possess her twin sister, Terri. [Possession]

257. Logan, Les. **Unnatural Talent**. New York: Bantam, 1983. 166pp. ISBN 0-553-23607-5. (Dark Forces series). **A**

Andrew desperately wants to please his father, the high school coach, by becoming a super basketball player. He even performs a magical rite from an old book of spells, only to find he must pay an awful price for becoming a basketball whiz. [Evil]

258. Lovecraft, H. P. **The Best of H. P. Lovecraft: Bloodcurdling Tales of Horror and the Macabre**. New York: Ballantine/Del Rey, 1983. 375pp. ISBN 0-345-29468-8. **C**
Movies inspired by Lovecraft's work: *Re-Animator:* 1985. Director: Stuart Gordon. Stars: Jeffrey Combs and Barbara Crampton. *From Beyond:* 1986. Director: Stuart Gordon. Stars: Jeffrey Combs, Barbara Crampton, and Ken Foree.

A collection of some of Lovecraft's best known tales, edited by Robert Bloch, the popular horror writer. Lovecraft is credited with creating the notion of the "Necromium," a long-forgotten book of occult Arab lore, as well as the often imitated theme of horrible monsters living in the bowels of the earth, often referred to as the Cthulhu Mythos. This collection includes "The Rats in the Walls," "The Picture in the House," "The Outsider," "Pickman's Model," "In the Vault," "The Silver Key," "The Music of Erich Zann," "The Call of Cthulhu," "The Dunwich Horror," "The Whisperer in Darkness," "The Colour Out of Space," "The Haunter of the Dark," "The Thing on the Doorstep," "The Shadow Over Innsmouth," "The Dreams in the Witch-House," "The Shadow out of Time." [Short stories]

259. MacAvoy, R. A. **Book of Kells**. New York: Bantam, 1985. 340pp. ISBN 0-553-25260-7. **C**

John Thornburn loves Ireland. One day he is transported back in time to an earlier, more magical time in that country, where he falls in love and goes on an important quest. [Magic; Time travel]

260. MacAvoy, R. A. **Damiano**. New York: Bantam, 1985. 243pp. ISBN 0-553-17154-2. **C**
   Sequels: *Damiano's Lute; Raphael.*

Damiano is a wizard's son and alchemist, but his fever to learn makes him a scholar and musician, as well. His dreams of a peaceful life in Renaissance Italy, learning to play the lute from the angel Raphael, are not to be, for he finds that he alone can save his home city from the destruction of invading troops. [Angels; Magic]

261. MacAvoy, R. A. **Tea with the Black Dragon**. New York: Bantam, 1983. 166pp. ISBN 0-553-23205-3. **A**
   Sequel: *Twisting the Rope.*

A contemporary woman seeks help from an oriental gentleman who claims to have magical powers vested in his 1,000-year-old black dragon. [Dragons; Magic]

262. McCammon, Robert R. **Mystery Walk**. New York: Ballantine, 1983. 419pp. ISBN 0-345-31514-6. (First published by Holt, 1983). **C**
   Other works: *Baal; They Thirst; The Night Beat; Bethany's Sin; Swan Song.*

Billy's Choctaw heritage may have given him strange and wonderful powers, but it has also given him the ability to know he is being pursued by the dreaded shape changer. [Paranormal abilities; Shamanism]

263. McCammon, Robert R. **Usher's Passing**. New York: Ballantine, 1985. 416pp. ISBN 0-345-32407-2. (First published by Holt, Rinehart and Winston, 1984). **C**

Suppose that Poe's famous tale of the House of Usher was true, or at least partly true? What if the Usher family still lives, possessed of great power, but with the ancient curse still very much a part of all their lives? [Evil; Haunted houses]

264. McDowell, Michael. **Blackwater I: The Flood**. New York: Avon, 1983. 189pp. ISBN 0-380-81489-7. **C**
   Sequels: *Blackwater II; Blackwater III; Blackwater IV; Blackwater V; Blackwater VI.*

A devastating flood immobilizes a small Alabama town in the early twentieth century. Elinor, a fascinating stranger with unusual powers, is found in the middle of the destruction, and she decides to stay and become a member of the community. Her odd habits cause comment, however. And the townspeople don't know a lot about her secret activities. [Transformation]

265. McIntyre, Vonda N. **The Bride**. New York: Dell, 1985. 221pp. ISBN 0-440-10801-2. **C**
   Other works: *Dreamsnake.* (See also entry 276.)
   Movie version: 1985. Director: Franc Roddam. Stars: Sting, Jennifer Beals, Geraldine Page, and Clancy Brown.

After Frankenstein creates his famous monster, he decides to perfect his skills and create a more delicate, beautiful model intended as the bride for his original creation. But he is so successful that he falls in love with her himself. [Monsters; Science gone wrong]

MacKay, Mary Mills. *See* Corelli, Marie.

266. McKillip, Patricia A. **The House on Parchment Street**. New York: Aladdin, 1978. 192pp. ISBN 0-689-70451-8. (First published by Atheneum, 1973). **B**

An American girl arrives to spend time with her English relatives in their 300-year-old house. Soon Carol and her English cousin, Bruce, find ghosts in the cellar. But there must be a reason why the ghosts are appearing only to them. [Ghosts]

267. McKinley, Robin. **Beauty**. New York: Pocket Books, 1985. 247pp. ISBN 0-671-60434-1. (First published by Harper & Row, 1978). **A**
Other works: *Imaginary Lands; The Blue Sword; The Hero and the Crown.*

A retelling of the story of Beauty and the Beast for today's teens, with a believable, matter-of-fact heroine who loves horses. [Fairy tales; Magic; Monsters]

268. McKinley, Robin. **The Door in the Hedge**. New York: Ace, 1982. 216pp. ISBN 0-441-15314-3. (First published by William Morrow, 1981). **A**

Four long fairy stories written in a matter-of-fact style include "The Stolen Princess;" "The Princess and the Frog;" "The Hunting of the Hind;" "The Twelve Dancing Princesses." [Fairy tales; Short stories]

269. MacLeod, Charlotte. **The Curse of the Giant Hogweed**. New York: Avon, 1986. 168pp. ISBN 0-380-70051-4. (First published by Doubleday, 1985). **C**

Professor Peter Shandy and his horticulture buddies from Balaclava College find themselves whisked from the United States back to ancient Wales where magic and legendary figures are real. Will Peter be able to cope in his new setting? Will he be stuck there forever? [Legends, Celtic; Magic]

270. McNally, Clare. **Ghost House**. New York: Bantam, 1979. 214pp. ISBN 0-440-18244-8. (First published by Doubleday, 1979?). **C**
Sequel: *Ghost House Revenge.*

When the VanBurens move to their new house, they little suspect that it was the home of a woman burned for witchcraft in an earlier time, or the terror that awaits them. [Haunted houses]

271. Mahy, Margaret. **The Changeover: A Supernatural Romance**. New York: Scholastic, 1985. 224pp. ISBN 0-590-33798-X. (First published by Atheneum, 1984). **A**
Other works: *Alien in the Family.*

Jacko, Laura's beloved younger brother, is being drained of his strength by a demon, and Laura turns to a teenage male witch to help save him. She learns, however, that she must pay a high price, that of becoming a witch herself. A story of courage and love set in contemporary New Zealand. [Witchcraft]

272. Mahy, Margaret. **The Haunting**. London: Magnet, 1984. 135pp. ISBN 0-416-48420-4. (First published by Methuen, 1982). **B**

Barney is frightened when the ghostly spirit of a young boy appears to him, the spirit of his assumed-dead great-uncle. But then he discovers that Great-uncle Cole is still alive. Barney must face some very strange truths about his mysterious family before the end of the story. [Paranormal abilities]

273. Marlin, J. **Getting out the Ghost**. New York: Pacer, 1984. 128pp. ISBN 0-399-21130-6. **B**

Joyce is an insecure teenager until the spirit of Gretta Marie enters her body, and Joyce becomes talented, smart, and popular. Then Gretta Marie starts doing things that Joyce doesn't like, but getting rid of Gretta Marie seems to be an impossible task. [Possession]

274. Martin, George R. **Fevre Dream**. New York: Pocket Books, 1983. 390pp. ISBN 0-671-43185-4. (First published by Poseidon Press, 1982). **C**
Other works: *Sandkings.*

A steamboat captain on the Mississippi finds that his mysterious backer, Joshua York, has embarked on a mission to save York's fellow vampires from their blood-drinking habits and free them from the rapacious blood-master. [Vampires]

275. Martin, Jack (pseud. of Dennis Etchison). **Halloween III: The Season of the Witch**. New York: Jove, 1982. 228pp. ISBN 0-515-08594-4. **C**
Movie version: 1982. Director: Tommy Lee Wallace. Stars: Tom Atkins, Stacey Nelkin, and Dan O'Herlihy.

The hypnotic television and radio commercial is driving parents crazy. Little do they realize that the halloween masks being sold have the power to destroy their children. [Evil; Horror]

276. Martin, Les. **The Bride**. New York: Random House, 1985. 93pp. ISBN 0-394-87370-X. **A**
Movie version: See item 265.

When Dr. Frankenstein produces a beautiful artificial woman as an intended bride for his famous monster, things don't work out as originally planned. She is such an improvement over the original model that the doctor falls in love with her himself. [Monsters; Science gone wrong]

277. Martin, Russ. **The Education of Jennifer Parrish**. New York: TOR, 1984. 319pp. ISBN 0-812-52154-4. **C**
Other works: *The Desecration of Susan Browning; The Possession of Jessica Young; The Obsession of Sally Wing.*

Students at a coed military prep school become the potential new bodies for the corrupt old members of the Organization who seek to dominate the world through evil. [Satanism; Transformation]

278. Marzolla, Jean. **Halfway Down Paddy Lane**. New York: Scholastic, 1984. 165pp. ISBN 0-590-33296-1. (First published by Dial, 1981). **B**

When Kate goes to sleep one night in an old house, she doesn't expect to wake up in an earlier time. Yet she does. In nineteenth century Massachusetts she learns what it's like to work in a textile mill and fall in love with the young man who believes he is her brother. [Time travel]

279. Masterton, Graham. **Death Trance**. New York: TOR, 1986. 409pp. ISBN 0-812-52187-0. **C**
Other works: *Charnel House; The Devils of D-Day; The Djinn; Ikon; The Manitou; The Pariah; Revenge of the Manitou; Tengu; The Sphinx.*

Randolph Clare is devastated when his wife and children are murdered. In his efforts to ease his grief, he asks an Indonesian physician to help him enter the realm of the dead in order to say goodbye. The physician warns him of the terrible dangers of such a journey, but Randolph does not heed him until it is too late. [Evil; Horror]

280. Masterton, Graham. **Picture of Evil**. New York: TOR, 1985. 379pp. ISBN 0-812-52199-4. **C**

An updated version of themes described by Wilde in *The Picture of Dorian Gray* (see item 445). Jet-set brother and sister from the Connecticut Gray family must scout out fresh young living skins to preserve their rotting bodies as they seek an old family portrait. [Evil]

281. Masterton, Graham. **The Wells of Hell**. New York: TOR, 1982. 317pp. ISBN 0-523-48042-3. (First published by Pocket Books, 1980). **C**

Horrible evil stalks a small New England town in the Lovecraft tradition. Children start to disappear, but are they really gone, or hiding in terror because they have become horrible, shell-encased monsters? [Evil; Monsters; Transformation]

Names beginning with "Mc," are filed as if "Mac."

282. Meany, Dee Morrison. **Iseult**. New York: Ace Fantasy, 1985. 229pp. ISBN 0-441-373887-9. **C**

Tristan, the virtuous knight was honored in King Arthur's court, but when he meets his uncle's beautiful wife, his honor seems a small price to pay for ecstasy. [Arthurian legends]

283. Merritt, Abraham. **Seven Footprints to Satan**. New York: Avon, 1942. 192pp. (First published by Boni & Liveright, 1928). **C**
Other works: *The Moon Pool; The Ship of Ishtar; The Face in the Abyss; Dwellers in the Mirage; Burn, Witch, Burn!; Thru the Dragon Glass; Creep, Shadow!; Three Lines of Old French; The Metal Monster; The Fox Woman and Other Stories.*

Dashing American heroes have long served as protagonists of pulp fiction. Here, James Kirkham, a daring explorer, takes on the ultimate foe—Satan, himself. It is up to Kirkham to save the souls and lives of others as well as himself and the beautiful woman of his dreams. [Evil; Satanism]

284. Merritt, Abraham, and Hannes Bok. **The Black Wheel**. New York: Avon, 1981. 296pp. ISBN 0-380-55822. (First published by New Collectors' Group, 1947). **C**

Composed from a fragment left at Merritt's death, the plot involves the plight of shipwrecked survivors, à la "Gilligan's Island." This, however, is no comedy, for the mismatched survivors soon discover they are not alone on the island, and an old wrong will come to terrorize them. The final climax is breathtaking, as horrible ghouls pursue the hero through endless, underground caves. [Curses; Zombies]

285. Meyrink, Gustav. **The Golem**. New York: Dover, 1976. 190pp. ISBN 0-486-25025-3. (First published in the United States by Houghton Mifflin, 1928). **D**

A mysterious and obtruse story dwelling on the meaning of reality. [Legends, Jewish]

286. Michaels, Barbara. **Ammie, Come Home**. New York: Fawcett, 1979. 223pp. ISBN 0-449-23926-8. (First published by Meredith, 1968). **C**
Other works: *The Walker in Shadows; Prince of Darkness; The Wizard's Daughter.*

Ruth Bennett is a widow, living a placid existence in her old Georgetown home, until the presence of others revives an old tragedy. Ruth must then help lay some ghosts to rest. [Ghosts]

287. Michaels, Barbara. **Here I Stay**. New York: TOR, 1985. 317pp. ISBN 0-812-52250-8. (First published by Congdon & Weed, 1983). **C**

Andrea was excited and exhausted as she and her husband, Jim, seem finally to have realized their dream of running an old country inn in Maryland. The old family house is full of quaint charm, but Andrea hadn't realized that there is an unexpected extra—a ghost. [Ghosts; Haunted houses]

288. Michaels, Philip. **Come, Follow Me**. New York: Avon, 1983. 328pp. ISBN 0-380-83006-X. **C**

Who is the evil musician who holds such power over children? Is he the Pied Piper of Hamlin, returned to earth for a more sinister purpose? [Evil]

289. Miller, J. P. **The Skook**. New York: Warner, 1984. 307pp. ISBN 0-446-32861-8. **C**

The Skook is an imaginary beast, made up to entertain Span Barrman's kids when they were young. When Span desperately needs help after being trapped in a huge underground cavern, the Skook turns up again, this time for real. But Span isn't sure the Skook will be much help. [Monsters]

290. Minton, T. M. **Offerings**. New York: Leisure, 1986. 395pp. ISBN 0-8439-2370-9. **C**

A group of dauntless scientists brave the primitive world of Oceania to investigate rumors of a living "missing link." Once there, however, they discover bestial "humans" who demand human sacrifices for their bloodthirsty god. [Legends, Oceanic]

291. Monaco, Richard. **Journey to the Flame**. New York: Bantam, 1985. 260pp. ISBN 0-553-25373-5. **C**
Sequel to: *She* by H. Rider Haggard (see item 167).

The author of *She* becomes a character in this new sequel to the famous tale of a fascinating, magical kingdom in Africa ruled by a dynamic, powerful, and beautiful woman. [Eternal life; Lost worlds]

292. Monette, Paul. **Nosferatu: The Vampyre**. New York: Avon, 1979. 172pp. ISBN 0-380-44107-1. **C**
Movie version: 1979. Director: Werner Herzog. Stars: Klaus Kinski, Isabelle Adjani, and Bruno Ganz.

A brooding version of the old classic about the immortal vampire. [Vampires]

293. Mordane, Thomas. **Bloodroot**. New York: Dell, 1982. 285pp. ISBN 0-440-10411-4. **C**

Quaint New England villages often have gnarled old oak trees, as well as odd customs practiced by the locals. Laura and Mark Avery learn to their horror, however, that their dream of a peaceful and productive life with a growing family in such a town is not to be. [Evil]

294. Morrell, David. **The Totem**. New York: Fawcett, 1979. 255pp. ISBN 0-449-20856-7. **C**

Potter's Field, Wyoming, is a poky little western town, that is, until the strange deaths and the growing terror overcome the people in the community. [Horror]

295. Mueller, Richard. **Ghostbusters: The Supernatural Spectacular**. New York: TOR, 1985. 250pp. ISBN 0-812-58598-4. **A**
Movie version: 1984. Director: Ivan Reitman. Stars: Bill Murray, Dan Ackroyd, Harold Ramis, Sigourney Weaver, and Rick Moranis.

When a bunch of ne'er-do-well scientists band together to eliminate ghosts, they never dream they'll run into evil entities so powerful they may be beyond even the skills of the Ghostbusters. [Ghosts]

296. Mundy, Talbot. **OM, the Secret of Ahbor Valley**. New York: Carroll & Graf, 1984. 392pp. ISBN 0-88184-045-9. (First published by Crown, 1924). **C**
Other works: *King of the Khyber Rifles.*

It is rumored that hidden deep in the Indian hills there is a holy lama who can reveal the secrets of the universe. It is also rumored that somewhere is a piece of jade with great supernatural powers. In the 1920s, a reckless young Englishman sets out to find the jade, and discovers many other things on his journey. [Legends, Tibetan; Mysticism]

297. Munn, H. Warner. **Merlin's Ring**. New York: Ballantine/Del Rey, 1981. 366pp. ISBN 0-345-24010-3. **C**
Other works: *Merlin's Godson.*

A sweeping fantasy from Atlantis to the discovery of America, in which Merlin's godson is involved in many mythological and historical adventures. Gwalchmai meets Corenice in ancient Atlantis, and their love endures through all. [Arthurian legends; Atlantis]

Munro, H. H. *See* Saki.

298. Nathan, Robert. **Portrait of Jennie**. New York: Dell, 1977. 124pp. (First published by Knopf, 1940). **C**
Movie version: 1948. Director: William Dieterle. Stars: Jennifer Jones, Joseph Cotten, and Ethel Barrymore.

A poor, struggling artist meets and paints the portrait of an enchanting girl named Jennie. Every time he meets Jennie, however, she has become much older, for, as she tells him, she has to catch up with him. [Time travel]

299. Naylor, Phyllis R. **The Witch's Sister**. New York: Aladdin, 1980. 160pp. ISBN 0-689-70471-2. (First published by Atheneum, 1975). **A**

Mrs. Tuggle is a most peculiar neighbor, young Lynn and her friend, Mouse, agree. In fact, they think she's a witch. Lynn is frightened for her sister, Judith, who seems to find Mrs. Tuggle fascinating and is taking lessons from her. She says they're dancing lessons, but Lynn thinks they may be lessons in witchcraft. [Witchcraft]

300. Neiderman, Andrew. **Night Howl**. New York: Pocket Books, 1986. 277pp. ISBN 0-671-60634-4. **C**
Other works: *Someone's Watching; Imp; Brainchild; Love Child.*

Little Bobby and his dog are faithful friends and companions until the day King turns vicious and has to be destroyed. But Bobby doesn't forget his old friend and sees him first in his dreams, then everywhere. Everyone in town becomes aware of King, for the dog has been turned into a monster of revenge. [Horror; Science gone wrong]

301. Neill, Robert. **Witch Bane**. London: Arrow, 1968. 224pp. (First published by Hutchinson, 1967). **C**
Other works include: *The Devil's Door*.

England's Civil War was full of brutality and hardship as neighbors fought each other, and the religious fervour of the Cromwellian forces became a harsh cleanser of evil in the land. Young Mary Standen is accused of being a witch. Although she is rescued by Major Dick Rowley, will she survive the turmoil of the times? [Witchcraft]

302. Netter, Susan. **Storm Child**. New York: Dell, 1983. 150pp. ISBN 0-440-98289-8. (Twilight series). **A**

When Cindy first gets a job as a mother's helper, she is pleased and excited. She'll get to spend the summer at a posh resort and her charge, Ian, seems easy to deal with. As the summer progresses, however, Cindy finds that Ian has an amazing power which becomes related, somehow, to the violent thunderstorms in the area. [Paranormal abilities]

303. Newman, Sharan. **Guinevere**. New York: St. Martin's, 1981. 257pp. ISBN 0-312-35321-9. (Zodiac Club series). **C**
Sequels: *Guinevere Evermore; The Chessboard Queen*.

Guinevere is a cherished young lady who even has her own unicorn. When she reluctantly grows up, however, she must face reality in the person of smitten young Arthur who wants to make her his queen. [Arthurian legends]

304. Nichols, Lynn J. **Taurus Trouble**. New York: Pacer, 1984. 160pp. ISBN 0-399-21109-8. **A**

Cathy is pleased by her chance to work at the local newspaper. She realizes, however, that her Leo sign and that of her nemesis, Danny Burns—a Taurus—mean a lot of conflict. [Astrology]

305. Nixon, Joan Lowery. **A Deadly Game of Magic**. New York: Laurel-Leaf, 1985. 148pp. ISBN 0-440-92102-3. (First published by Harcourt Brace Jovanovich, 1983). **A**
Other works include: *The Seance; The Specter*.

When four children take refuge in a mysterious house, they soon realize that the dangers of the storm outside are nothing compared to the bizarre happenings inside. [Legerdemain; Magic]

306. Norton, Andrew, and Phyllis Miller. **House of Shadows**. New York: TOR, 1985. 250pp. ISBN 0-812-54743-8. (First published by Atheneum, 1984). **A**

The old house seems full of secrets. Susan finds herself having dreams of the children who lived in the house many years ago, children who had met a savage fate at the hands of vengeful Indians. Although those things happened in the past, Susan discovers that magic can make past events repeat themselves, and finds herself in great danger. [Legends, Native American; Magic]

307. Nye, Robert. **Beowulf: a New Telling**. New York: Laurel-Leaf, 1982. 96pp. ISBN 0-686-85864-6. (First published by Hill & Wang, 1968). **D**
Other works: *Merlin*.

A modernized version of the Beowulf legend, which describes the adventures of a hero opposing the monsters Grendel and his mother. [Monsters]

308. Oates, Joyce Carol. **Night-Side**. New York: Fawcett/Crest, 1977. 318pp. ISBN 0-449-24206-4. **C**
Other works: *Bellefleur*.

Intricate, mysterious stories by a highly respected American writer include "Night-Side," "The Windows," "Lover," "The Snowstorm," "The Translation," "The Dungeon," "Famine Country," "Bloodstains," "Exile," "The Giant Woman," "Daisy," "The Murder," "Fatal Woman," "The Sacrifice," "The Thaw," "Further Confessions," "The Blessing," "A Theory of Knowledge." [Short stories]

309. O'Brien, Fitz-James. **The Fantastic Tales of Fitz-James O'Brien**. London: Calder, 1977. 149pp. ISBN 0-7145-3617-2. **D**

Edited by Michael Hayes, these supernatural stories by a nineteenth century author include "The Diamond Lens," "The Lost Room," "What Was It?" "The Wondersmith," "Seeing the World," "The Pot of Tulips," "The Dragon Fang Possessed by the Conjurer Piou-Lu." [Short stories]

310. Orgill, Douglas, and John Gribbin. **Brother Esau**. New York: TOR, 1984. 288pp. ISBN 0-8125-8680-8. (First published by Harper & Row, 1983). **C**

Suppose somebody really finds an abominable snowman? Dr. Liliane Erckmann and her team of scientists do, and find there are great problems in making such a great discovery. [Abominable snowman]

311. Paige, Richard (pseud. of Dean R. Koontz). **The Door to December**. New York: Signet, 1985. 405pp. ISBN 0-451-13605-5. **C**

An exciting tale of pursuit and mystery, throughout which Dr. Laura McCaffrey tries to bring her daughter, Melanie, back from the catatonic state induced by behavior modification experiments. [Altered states of consciousness]

312. Palatini, Margie. **Capricorn & Co**. New York: Pacer, 1984. 160pp. ISBN 0-399-21186-1. (Zodiac Club series). **A**

The members of the Zodiac Club are very close friends, as Gail finds out when she starts to experiment with a new business with her boyfriend. Her plans don't include her Zodiac buddies, and that means trouble. Includes appropriate gift ideas for every zodiac sign. [Astrology]

313. Palatini, Margie. **Scorpio's Class Act**. New York: Pacer, 1985. 160pp. ISBN 0-425-08406-X. (Zodiac Club series). **A**

None of the Zodiac Club members is from really exclusive families, but when J. L. gets a chance to date Chad she considers leaving her old friends behind and joining a high society set. Includes gem stones for every zodiac sign. [Astrology]

314. Pascal, Francine. **Hangin' Out with Cici**. New York: Archway, 1978. 231pp. ISBN 0-671-43879-4. New York: Laurel-Leaf, 1985. 160pp. ISBN 0-440-93364-1. (First published by Viking, 1977). **A**

Thirteen-year-old Victoria thinks her mother, Cici, doesn't understand her. When Victoria travels back in time, she finds herself best friends with her own mother as they engage in adventures together. And Cici seems to get into worse trouble than Victoria ever dreamed possible! [Time travel]

315. Payne, Bernal C., Jr. **Trapped in Time**. New York: Archway, 1986. 151pp. ISBN 0-671-54360-1. (First published as *It's about Time* by Macmillan, 1984). **A**

You have to be careful about traveling in time. You must never disturb the past, for it may change the future. Gail and Chris find this out the hard way when they travel back in time to meet their own parents as teenagers. [Time travel]

316. Pearce, Philippa. **The Shadow-Cage: And Other Tales of the Supernatural**. Harmondsworth, England: Puffin, 1978. 151pp. ISBN 0-14-03-1073-8. (First published by Kestrel, 1977). **B**

An English author describes strange goings-on in stories which include "The Shadow-Cage;" "Miss Mountain;" "Guess;" "At the River-Gates;" "Her Father's Attic;" "The Running-Companion;" "Beckoned;" "The Dear Little Man with His Hands in His Pockets;" "The Dog Got Them;" "The Strange Illness of Mr. Arthur Cook." [Short stories]

317. Pearlman, Gilbert. **Young Frankenstein**. New York: Ballantine, 1974. 152pp. ISBN 345-24268-8. **A**
      Movie version: 1974. Director: Mel Brooks. Stars: Gene Wilder, Peter Boyle, Marty Feldman, Teri Garr, and Madeline Kahn.

Freddy Frankenstein has just received word that he is the "lucky" heir to the Frankenstein estate, a great disappointment to his various weird relatives who lust after the family fortune. All Freddy has to do is take possession, which turns out to be quite an arduous task. [Monsters; Science gone wrong]

318. Peck, Richard. **The Ghost Belonged To Me**. New York: Laurel-Leaf, 1983. 253pp. ISBN 0-440-93075-8. (First published by Viking, 1977). **A**
      Sequels: *Ghosts I Have Been; The Dreadful Future of Blossom Culp; Blossom Culp and the Sleep of Death.*

Blossom Culp is a delightful, irrepressible youngster living (and trying to survive in school) just prior to World War I. Her tales of her amazing family (her mother is a gypsy with the sight) and her own abilities to see more than others make her a notorious character with her classmates. Blossom doesn't care, except when it comes to Alexander, because she really wants to be his friend. [Paranormal abilities]

319. Perl, Lila. **Annabelle Starr, E.S.P.** New York: Archway, 1984. 134pp. ISBN 0-671-50350-2. (First published by Clarion, 1983). **B** Other works include: *Marleen, the Horror Queen.*

Annabelle discovers she has secret, psychic abilities, but she is uncertain if this power will be enough to protect her brother, Scott, from being taken away from her. [Paranormal abilities]

320. Pevsner, Stella. **Footsteps on the Stairs.** New York: Archway, 1984. 150pp. ISBN 0-671-52411-9. (First published by Simon & Schuster, 1970). **B**

Experimenting with ESP is fun, but Chip and his friends discover that there aren't always scientific explanations for all that happens. In fact, it seems as if there may be some real ghosts involved. [Ghosts]

321. Poe, Edgar Allan. **The Tell-Tale Heart and Other Writings.** New York: Bantam, 1982. 432pp. ISBN 0-553-21575-2. **C** Movies versions of Poe's works include: *House of Usher:* 1960. Director: Roger Corman. Stars: Vincent Price, Mark Damon, and Myrna Fahey. *The Fall of the House of Usher:* 1982. Director: James L. Conway. Stars: Martin Landau, Robert Hays, and Charlene Tilton. *The Mask of the Red Death:* 1964. Director: Roger Corman. Stars: Vincent Price, Hazel Court, and Jane Asher. *The Pit and the Pendulum:* 1961. Director: Roger Corman. Stars: Vincent Price, John Kerr, and Barbara Steele. *The Tomb of Ligeia:* 1964. Director: Roger Corman. Stars: Vincent Price, Elizabeth Shepherd, and John Westbrook.

An assortment of tales by the American master including "The Tell-Tale Heart," "The Black Cat," "The Cask of Amontillado," "The Fall of the House of Usher," "The Masque of the Red Death," "The Facts in the Case of M. Valdemar," "Ligeia," "The Murders in the Rue Morgue," "The Purloined Letter," "A Descent into the Maelstrom," "The Pit and the Pendulum," "Ms. Found in a Bottle," "The Premature Burial," "William Wilson," "Eleonora," "Silence — A Fable," "The Narrative of Arthur Gordon Pym." [Short stories]

322. Pope, Elizabeth Marie. **The Perilous Gard.** New York: Tempo, 1984. 211pp. ISBN 0-441-65956-X. (First published by Houghton Mifflin, 1974). **A**

Kate is a spirited young damsel who is banished from the royal court by an angry Queen Mary. She is sent to a mysterious castle in the windswept north, where she discovers the secret kingdom of the faeries. Not only does she discover the elusive, legendary beings, she becomes their prisoner. [Fairies]

323. Pope, Elizabeth Marie. **The Sherwood Ring**. New York: Tempo, 1985. 180pp. ISBN 0-441-76111-9. (First published by Houghton, Mifflin, 1958). **A**

When Peggy first visits her family's ancestral home in upstate New York, she thinks she'll find interesting old antiques, not the ghostly secrets of the past. [Ghosts]

324. Potocki, Jan. **The Saragossa Manuscript**. New York: Avon, 1961. 224pp. (First published in Paris, 1804). **C**

Gothic tales of mystery and adventure. Includes a series of tales in the tradition of Chaucer and Boccaccio, all with a supernatural twist. [Short stories]

325. Prince, Alison. **The Ghost Within**. London: Magnet, 1986. 119pp. ISBN 0-416-52140-1. (First published by Methuen, 1984). **A**

Stories of odd happenings, most with English settings, including "The Lilies," "Herb," "The Fire Escape," "Photographs," "The Fen Tiger," "Dundee Cake," "The Pin," "The Glass Game." [Short stories]

326. Prose, Francine. **Marie Laveau**. New York: Berkley, 1977. 374pp. ISBN 425-03727-4. **C**

Living outside the fringes of respectable New Orlean's society, beautiful and powerful Marie Laveau was able to exert her will on everyone she pleased with voodoo spells and power. [Voodoo]

327. Ptacek, Kathryn. **Kachina**. New York: TOR, 1986. 306pp. ISBN 0-812-52445-4. **C**
Other works: *Blood Autumn*.

A properly reared young lady starts to have strange dreams on a trip to the New Mexico territory. Her anthropologist husband seems unconcerned about Elizabeth, as she finds her dreams becoming more and more real. Finally she finds herself becoming the vengeful leader of the Konochine tribe. [Evil; Legends, Native American; Shamanism]

328. Ptacek, Kathryn. **Shadoweyes**. New York: TOR, 1984. 314pp. ISBN 0-812-51858-6. **C**

Terrible, rapacious, evil beings called shadoweyes are on a rampage eating animal and human flesh. Can Chato Del-Klinne, the Apache hero, save the world from this horrible menace? [Horror]

329. Ramie, Florence. **Toyland**. New York: Leisure, 1986. 395pp. ISBN 0-8439-2391-1. **C**

The MacKenzie family appear to be one of the most ordinary American families around. But strange things are going on in their house—things which promise knowledge of dark secrets from the past. [Ghosts; Horror]

330.   Ramsay, Jay. **Night of the Claw**. New York: TOR, 1985. 367pp. ISBN 0-812-52500-0. **C**

A gruesome tale of child murder and cannibalism. Not for the squeamish. [Cults; Legends, Primitive]

331.   Read, Cameron. **The Forsaken**. New York: Pinnacle, 1982. 343pp. ISBN 0-523-41595-8. **C**

The Hamilton family lives in a beautiful old North Carolina house, but there is something strange about the noises in the evening when people try to go to sleep. A gentle story, reportedly based on a true ghost experience. [Ghosts; Haunted houses]

332.   Reed, Ishmael. **Mumbo Jumbo**. New York: Avon/Bard, 1978. 256pp. ISBN 0-380-01860-8. (First published by Doubleday, 1972). **C**
Other works: *A Secretary to the Spirits; The Freelance Paulbearers.*

An outrageous and original work dealing with HooDoo (voodoo). Whether or not it is real or fantasy is left to the reader to decide. [Voodoo]

333.   Rees, E. M. **Gemini Solo**. New York: Pacer, 1985. 160pp. ISBN 0-448-47727-0. (Zodiac Club series). **A**

Ann Crawford finds her new friends are great after the family moves to Connecticut, but she miscalculates when she fixes her twin brother up with Abby, the founder of the Zodiac Club. Includes the perfect places to live for each zodiac sign. [Astrology]

334.   Rees, E. M. **Libra's Dilemma**. New York: Pacer, 1984. 160pp. ISBN 0-399-21108-X. (Zodiac Club series). **A**

Librans have a strong sense of fair play, and Mara's is solely tested when she discovers her boyfriend is involved in a cheating scandal. Includes food ideas for the zodiac signs. [Astrology]

335.   Rees, E. M. **Pisces Times Two**. New York: Pacer, 1985. 160pp. ISBN 0-448-47731-9. (Zodiac Club series). **A**

When her father presents her with a new stepmother, Elizabeth decides their house just isn't big enough for two temperamental Pisces. Includes the right dog for every zodiac sign. [Astrology]

336.   Renault, Mary. **The King Must Die**. New York: Bantam, 1974. 416pp. ISBN 0-553-26065-0. (First published by Pantheon, 1958). **C**
Sequel: *The Bull from the Sea.*
Other works: *Last of the Wine.*

An exciting, detailed portrayal of life in ancient Greece based on the legend of Theseus. [Legends, Classical]

337. Rice, Anne. **Interview with the Vampire**. New York: Ballantine, 1977. 346pp. ISBN 0-345-25608-5. (First published by Knopf, 1977). **C**
Sequel: *The Vampire, Lestat.*

The journey and adventures of a sympathetic vampire are recounted as he wanders from New Orleans to Europe in his search for happiness. [Vampires]

338. Rice, Jeff. **The Night Stalker**. New York: Pocket Books, c1973, 1974. 192pp. **C**
Movie version: 1971. Director: John Llewellyn Moxey. Stars: Darren McGavin and Carol Lynley. Later spin-off television series.

Las Vegas, that town of glitz and bright lights, seems an odd place to find a vampire. But a newspaper reporter, down on his luck, does find one, and discovers that getting others to believe in this occult murderer is very hard work indeed. [Vampires]

339. Rohmer, Sax (pseud. of Arthur Henry Ward). **The Insidious Dr. Fu Manchu**. New York: Zebra/Kensington, 1985. 331pp. ISBN 0-821-71668-9. (First published by Doubleday, 1939). **C**
Other works: *The Drums of Fu Manchu; The Trail of Fu Manchu; The Dreams of Fu Manchu.*
Movie versions of the Fu Manchu books include: *Face of Fu Manchu:* 1965. Director: Don Sharp. Stars: Christopher Lee, Nigel Green, and Tsai Chinn. *The Brides of Fu Manchu:* 1966. Director: Don Sharp. Stars: Christopher Lee, Douglas Wilner, and Marie Versini. *Vengeance of Fu Manchu:* 1968. Director: Jeremy Summers. Stars: Christopher Lee, Douglas Wilmer, and Tsai Chinn.

The evil villain makes full use of black magic and evil scientific practices to prolong his life and gain power. Only Nyland Grant of Scotland Yard is able to occasionally thwart the nefarious doctor, doggedly pursuing him through a tangled web of horror and danger. [Black magic]

Ross, Dan. *See* Ross, Marilyn.

340. Ross, Leona C. **Resurrexit**. New York: Leisure, 1986. 384pp. ISBN 0-8439-2331-8. **C**

All small towns have queer old ladies living in them, and Newton, Maine, is no exception. What people don't realize, however, is that Florence Willowby is more than a little odd; she is obsessed with the memories of her past which will drive her to anything, even human sacrifice. [Horror]

341. Ross, Marilyn (pseud. of Dan Ross). **Barnabas Collins**. New York: Paperback Library, 1968. 157pp. **C**
Sequels: Twenty-six additional titles, all based on the ABC television series, "Dark Shadows."
Movie version: *House of Dark Shadows:* 1970. Director: Dan Curtis. Stars: Jonathan Fried, Grayson Hall, and Kathryn Leigh Scott.

Barnabas Collins, an old (175 years old, in fact), but still handsome and fascinating vampire, comes to live in the old Collins house. His tragic eyes attract women, but the women do not realize the terrible secret he holds within himself. [Vampires]

342. Roueche, Berton. **Feral**. New York: Avon, 1983. 128pp. ISBN 0-380-65508-X. (First published by Harper & Row, 1974). **C**

A perfect resort house becomes a far-from-perfect residence of terror when countless wild creatures surround it, making the Bishops prisoners in their own home. [Evil; Monsters]

343. Rudorff, Raymond. **The Dracula Archives**. New York: Pocket Books, 1972. 208pp. ISBN 0-899-19436-2. (First published by Arbor House, 1971). **C**

A collection of documents, letters, diaries, and other memorabilia provide firm "proof" of Count Dracula's existence. [Vampires]

344. Rush, Allison. **The Last of Danu's Children**. New York: TOR, 1984. 315pp. ISBN 0-8125-5250-4. (First published by Houghton Mifflin, 1982). **A**

Ancient Celtic gods appear in modern England and affect the lives of three teenagers. Anna Marchant is especially affected, for she is stolen away by Cernunnos. Anna's sister, Kate, and Matt Cooper must try to save her, but even with the help of Danu's Children, born of Light, they may not be able to succeed. [Legends, Celtic]

345. Ryan, Alan. **The Kill**. New York: TOR, 1982. 312pp. ISBN 0-523-48055-5. **C**
Other works: *Dead White; Cast a Cold Eye; Panther!; Halloween Horrors.*

The private dream of many New Yorkers is to throw it all away and run to the idyllic beauties of the wooded Catskill Mountains. Jack and Megan, however, discover terror in the wooded darkness, an unbelievable horror that will destroy their happiness forever. [Horror]

346. Saberhagen, Fred. **Frankenstein Papers**. New York: Baen, 1986. 308pp. ISBN 0-671-65550-7. **C**
Other works: *The Holmes/Dracula File.*

The story of Frankenstein's creation from the monster's point of view. Who says that such a creation cannot have a soul? This "creation," alas, turns out to be an alien from outer space. [Monsters; Science gone wrong]

347. St. George, Judith. **Haunted**. New York: Bantam, 1982. 158pp. ISBN 0-553-20868-3. (First published by Putnam, 1980). **B**

Alex Phillip's summer of house sitting seems easy at first. Then weird things start to happen, and Alex is afraid that there are forces at work with which he won't be able to deal—forces that are not human. [Evil; Ghosts]

St. John, David. *See* Hunt, Howard E.

348. **St. John, Wylly Folk. The Ghost Next Door.** New York: Archway, 1972. 152pp. ISBN 0-671-55390-9. (First published by Simon & Schuster, 1971). **B**

When Sherry goes to visit her aunt in a quiet little Georgia town, people are puzzled when she talks about her playmate whom no one else can see. Then, other clues make the puzzlement turn to fear as people realize Sherry's friend may be long-dead Miranda, drowned in a desolate pond. [Ghosts]

349. **Saki (pseud. of Hector Hugh Munro). Humor, Horror, and the Supernatural: 22 Stories by Saki.** New York: Scholastic, n.d. 158pp. **C**

Clever and scary stories by a master teller of tales, including "Gabriel-Ernest," "The Bag," "Tobermory," "Mrs. Packletide's Tiger," "Sredni Vashtar," "The Easter Egg," "Filboid Studge," "Laura," "The Open Window," "The Schartz-Matterklume Method," "A Holiday Task," "The Storyteller," "The Name Day," "The Lumber Room," "The Disappearance of Crispina Umberleigh," "The Wolves of Cernograntz," "The Guests," "The Penance," "The Interlopers," "The Mappined Life," "The Seven Cream Jugs," "The Gala Programme." [Short stories]

350. **Saralegui, Jorge. Last Rites.** New York: Charter, 1985. 279pp. ISBN 0-441-47185-4. **C**

An evil beast is loose in charming San Francisco, and its power has insinuated itself into unsuspecting, innocent victims who turn to vile practices. [Horror; Vampires]

351. **Saul, John. Comes the Blind Fury.** New York: Dell, 1980. 384pp. ISBN 0-440-11475-6. **C**
Other works: *Brainchild; The God Project; Cry for the Strangers; Punish the Sinners; Suffer the Children; When the Wind Blows; Hell Fire.*

A blind child in the nineteenth century is taunted and hounded to her death by the other village children. The anger of the child lives on as an avenging spirit bound on seeking retribution. [Ghosts]

352. **Saul, John. Nathaniel.** New York: Bantam, 1984. 343pp. ISBN 0-553-24172-9. **C**

When young Michael's father dies, Michael and his pregnant mother return to his father's desolate family home. Michael soon discovers that someone, or something, is invading his mind. Can it be the spirit of Nathaniel, a long-dead child? Terror mounts as Michael's mother struggles to save her son. [Ghosts]

353. Saxon, Peter. **Dark Ways to Death**. London: Sphere, 1975. 140pp. ISBN 0-7221-7655-4. (First published by Baker, 1968). **C**
Other works: *Brother Blood; The Vampires of Finistere; Vampire Moon.*

A classic tale of good against evil. Can The Guardians, only five in all, summon enough strength to combat the powers of a dangerous voodoo cult, led by Doctor Obadiah Dubal? [Voodoo]

354. Scanlon, Noel. **Apparitions**. New York: Lorevan, 1986. 208pp. ISBN 0-931773-57-1. (First published by Robert Hale, 1984). **C**

A desolate Irish island is turned into a commune by the followers of Guru Pradavana. When one of their members dies, she is cremated on a funeral pyre. Then it is discovered that she really wasn't dead at all, merely in a trance and had been arbitrarily sacrificed to a greedy god. [Evil; Legends, Indian]

355. Scarborough, Elizabeth. **The Drastic Dragon of Draco, Texas**. New York: Bantam/Spectra, 1986. 247pp. ISBN 0-553-25887-7. **C**
Other works: *Browyn's Bane; The Unicorn Creed.*

Dragons are supposed to be long dead, or legendary, but in a little western town, a dragon is terrorizing the surrounding countryside. No one seems able to do anything about it, however, until Delores, a brave young woman, decides to tackle the beast. [Dragons]

356. Schoell, William. **Late at Night**. New York: Leisure, 1986. 382pp. ISBN 0-8439-2319-9. **C**
Other works: *Spawn of Hell.*

A group of young people foolishly gather for a weekend on Lammerty Island, long reputed to be haunted by terror and violence. One of the campers discovers an ancient book which describes their very own group perfectly, and then details how each of them will die by terrible means. Now the daring investigators realize their mistake in underestimating the powers of evil, for their lives may well be the price they pay. [Evil; Horror]

357. Schoell, William. **Shivers**. New York: Leisure, 1985. 398pp. ISBN 0-8439-2235-4. **C**

A horrible being is slowly taking over the city, picking as its first victims the weak and powerless. But its ultimate aim will touch everyone before it is done, for it is Prime Evil. [Evil; Horror]

358. Scott, R. C. **Blood Sport**. New York: Bantam, 1984. 144pp. ISBN 0-553-23866-3. (Dark Forces series). **A**

Bob Lindquist finds to his sorrow and horror that his infatuation with a beautiful girl has led him into a night world from which he cannot escape. [Evil]

359. Seltzer, David. **The Omen**. New York: Signet, 1976. 208pp. ISBN 0-451-11989-4. **C**
     Other works: *One Is a Lonely Number; The Other Side of the Mountain.*
     Sequels: *Damien: The Omen, Part II* by Joseph Howard; *The Final Conflict: Omen III* by Gordon McGill; *Omen IV: Armageddon 2000* by Gordon McGill; *Omen V: The Abomination* by Jack Mason.
     Movie version: 1976. Director: Richard Donner. Stars: Gregory Peck, Lee Remick, and David Warner.

     The devil's son has been born again, and his evil cannot be comprehended at first by his wealthy, loving parents. Eventually they come to see this child for what he is, but will they be able to stop him? [The devil]

360. Serling, Rod. **Stories from the Twilight Zone**. New York: Bantam, 1986. 418pp. ISBN 0-553-34329-7. **C**
     (See item 479.)
     Movie version: 1983. Directors: John Landis, Steven Spielberg, Joe Dante, and George Miller. Stars: Vic Morrow, Scatman Crothers, Kathleen Quinlan, Kevin McCarthy, and John Lithgow.

     Stories from the successful television series include "The Mighty Casey," "Escape Clause," "Walking Distance," "The Fever," "Where is Everybody? " "The Monsters Are Due on Maple Street," "The Lonely," "Mr. Dingle, the Strong," "A Thing about Machines," "The Big, Tall Wish," "A Stop at Willoughby," "The Odyssey of Flight," "Dust," "The Whole Truth," "The Shelter," "Showdown with Rance McGrew," "The Night of the Meek," "The Midnight Sun," "The Rip van Winkle Caper." [Short stories]

361. Setlowe, Richard. **The Haunting of Suzanna Blackwell**. New York: Signet, 1985. 298pp. ISBN 0-451-13556-3. **C**

     For years Suzanna has been comforted by the presence of her mother's ghost. Now, however, there are other ghosts in her life, and they threaten to destroy those relationships that are most important to her, as well as her own personality. [Ghosts; Possession]

362. Sharman, Nick. **The Switch**. New York: Signet, 1984. 287pp. ISBN 0-451-13102-9. **C**

     Trudy Lawrence is totally charmed by Mark Anderson. But then her old boy friend is killed and horrifying spectres start to appear. Trudy finds her life haunted and hideous. She may never be able to escape. [Evil; Ghosts]

363. Shecter, Ben. **Game for Demons**. New York: Trophy, 1972. 193pp. ISBN 06-440054-9. (First published by Harper & Row, 1972). **B**
     Other works: *The River Witches; Conrad's Castle.*

     All kids have trouble with school and family, but Gordie Cassman has problems that seem worse than usual. Not only does his mother seem all screwed up, his own mind seems to be going, too. [Demons]

364. Shelley, Mary. **Frankenstein**. New York: Bantam, 1981. 240pp. ISBN 0-553-21172-2. (First published by Lackington Hughes Hardin Mayor & Jones, 1818). **D**
Movie versions: 1931. Director: James Whale. Stars: Colin Clive, Mae Clarke, and Boris Karloff. *Frankenstein: The True Story:* 1973. Director: Jack Smight. Stars: James Mason, Leonard Whiting, Michael Sarrazin, and David McCallum.

The legendary tale of a scientist whose creation becomes more powerful and more human than his creator had intended. [Science gone wrong; Transformation]

365. Siegel, Scott. **The Companion**. New York: Bantam, 1983. 134pp. ISBN 0-553-23676-8. (Dark Forces series). **A**

Lots of children have secret, pretend friends, but Jeff's pal, Kim, has somehow materialized into a possessive, evil demon. [Demons]

366. Silverberg, Robert. **The Book of Skulls**. New York: Bantam, 1983. 196pp. ISBN 0-553-23057-3. (First published by Scribner's, 1972). **C**
Other works: *Lord Valentine's Castle.*

Four college students go on a pilgrimage to the House of Skulls, a place in the southwestern desert where an ancient brotherhood guards a powerful secret, the gift of eternal life. But there is a heavy price to be paid for the gift, for not all of the four will be permitted to live out their ordinary human life spans. [Eternal life]

367. Silverberg, Robert. **Gilgamesh the King**. New York: Bantam/Spectra, 1985. 306pp. ISBN 0-553-25250-X. (First published by Arbor House, 1984). **A**

A hero of ancient Sumeria, Gilgamesh, is part god, part man, and slayer of demons. This modernized version of a fascinating legend includes all the elements of a favorite epic: intrigue, quests, romance, and betrayal. [Legends, Sumerian]

368. Silverstone, Lou. **The Mad Book of Horror Stories, Yecchy Creatures, and Other Neat Stuff**. New York: Warner, 1986. 192pp. ISBN 0-446-32286-5. **A**

Horror comics in the zany style familiar to *Mad* readers, including "Gefilta—the Killer Carp," "The Horror Movie Hate Book," "The Curse of the Werewolf," "The Creatures that Come from the Headlines," "A Mad Look at Dracula," "That House in Vomityville," "The Fall of the House of Gusher," "Dr. Hackyl & Mr. High," "A Mad Look at Igor," "Camp Sleep-Away." [Short stories]

369. Simpson, George E., and Neal R. Burger. **Ghostboat**. New York: Dell, 1985. 412pp. ISBN 0-440-15421-9. (First published by Dell, 1976). **C**

Navy Commander Ed Frank is determined to find out why the submarine Candlefish, lost in 1944, has mysteriously returned. He embarks on a dangerous voyage to find the unspeakable truth and finds an incredible answer hidden deep in the ocean. [Disappearances]

370. Sinclair, Quinn. **The Boy Who Could Draw Tomorrow**. New York: Dell/Emerald, 1984. 221pp. ISBN 0-440-00745-3. **C**

Hal and Peggy Cooper have just decided their lives and careers are paying off. Both are doing well in their high-pressure jobs, well enough that they can afford to move to a better apartment on the affluent upper east side of New York. Their darling boy, Sam, is enrolled in the best private school around, and his future seems boundless. But the pictures Sam draws become more and more disturbing, and what's worse, the scenes in his pictures come true. [Paranormal abilities]

371. Singer, Isaac Bashevis. **The Magician of Lublin**. New York: Fawcett/Crest, 1980. 288pp. ISBN 0-449-20966-0. (First published by Farrar, Straus & Giroux, 1960). **C**
Movie version: 1979. Director: Menachen Golan. Stars: Alan Arkin, Louise Fletcher, Valerie Perrine, and Shelley Winters.

Yasha Mazur, the magician of Lublin, is a man of extraordinary talents, although not a hero in his own home town. He is more than a stage magician, for he can read minds and communicate with spirits. All in all, he is a man who is not destined to lead a common life. [Magic; Paranormal abilities]

372. Singer, Isaac Bashevis. **The Seance**. New York: Fawcett, 1981. 255pp. ISBN 0-449-24364-8. (First published by Farrar, Straus & Giroux, 1968). **C**

Tales of mystery by a master storyteller include "The Seance," "The Slaughterer," "The Dead Fiddler," "The Lecture," "Cockadoodledoo," "The Plagiarist," "Zeitl and Rickel," "The Warehouse," "Henne Fine," "Getzel the Monkey," "Yanda," "The Needle," "Two Corpses Go Dancing," "The Parrot," "The Brooch," "The Letter Writer." [Short stories]

373. Skipp, John, and Craig Spector. **The Light at the End**. New York: Bantam, 1986. 385pp. ISBN 0-553-25451-0. **C**

The Ancient One has come to New York to enlarge his evil clan. Rudy, his first victim, decides to become all-powerful himself. Rudy's friends are among his victims as he roams the subway tunnels and bizarre night world of Greenwich Village. A small force, however, gathers to stop Rudy before it is too late. Or is it too late already? [Vampires]

374. Sleator, William. **Blackbriar**. New York: Scholastic/Point, 1982. 217pp. ISBN 0-590-40308-7. (First published by Dutton, 1972). **A**
Other works: *House of Stairs; Singularity; Among the Dolls.*

Young Danny Chilton finds Blackbriar fascinating, even if it is a bit scary. His new friend, Lark, helps Danny discover the meaning behind the mystery, and it is far scarier than Danny had originally thought. It is bad enough when they find out that Blackbriar had once been a pesthouse, a place where plague victims were brought to die in earlier times, but the mysterious lights on a nearby hill hint at even worse secrets. [Witchcraft]

375. Sleator, William. **Into the Dream**. New York: Scholastic/Apple, n.d. 154pp. ISBN 0-590-33982-6. (First published by Dutton, 1979). **B**

Francine Gill and Paul Rhodes are having the same dream every night. The dream shows a mysterious, glowing object, a run-down motel, and a small boy in danger. Somehow Francine and Paul must stop a terrible horror from happening, even though they are in danger themselves. [Evil]

376. Sloane, Robert C. **A Nice Place to Live**. New York: Crown, 1981. 278pp. ISBN 0-517-545152. **C**
Other works: *The Vengeance.*

The Marinos think their new house is perfect. Then odd things start to happen, and Mr. Marino starts to behave very strangely. Can he be becoming someone else, or even *something* else? [Evil]

377. Smith, A. C. H. **Labyrinth**. New York: Holt/Owl, 1986. 183pp. ISBN 0-03-007322-4. **A**
Movie version: 1986. Director: Jim Henson. Stars: David Bowie and the Jim Henson puppets.

Courageous Sarah must tackle the dangers of the goblin world to try to save her little brother, Toby. If she is not in time, the fascinating goblin king, Jareth, will keep him forever. [Evil; Fairies]

378. Smith, Guy N. **The Neophyte**. London: New English Library, 1986. 3,112pp. ISBN 0-450-05858-1. **C**
Other works: *Killer Crabs; Night of the Crabs; The Origin of the Crabs; Crabs on the Rampage; Crabs' Moon; Son of the Werewolf; Wolfcurse; The Slime Beast; The Sucking Pit; Thirst; Bats out of Hell; Caracal; Warhead; Blood Circuit; The Undead; Accursed; The Walking Dead; Throwback; The Wood; The Graveyard Vultures; The Blood Merchants; Cannibal Cult; The Druid Connection.*

Joby is a witch-boy, and the villagers all hate the teenager, except for his loyal friend Ally and the mysterious, alluring, and fascinating Sally Ann. Sally Ann wants Joby because she also is a witch, but Joby wants no part of his heritage and fights desperately to gain his freedom. [Horror; Witchcraft]

379. Smith, Janet Patton. **The Twisted Room**. New York: Dell, 1983. 154pp. ISBN 0-440-98690-7. (Twilight series). **A**

When Lisa first spots the girl in the window next door, she wonders about her. She seems lonely and almost afraid, as if she is in trouble. Then Lisa, to her horror, finds out that Marie Worthington isn't alive any more. [Ghosts]

380. Smith, Martin Cruz. **Nightwing**. New York: Jove, 1977. 255pp. ISBN 0-515-06124-7. (First published by Norton, 1977). **C**
Movie version: 1979. Director: Arthur Hiller. Stars: Nick Mancuso, David Warner, and Kathryn Harrold.

The beauty of the southwestern desert becomes more and more fearsome as the power of rapacious superbats becomes more apparent to the leaders of the tribes in the area. [Monsters; Mysticism]

381. Smith, Thorne. **Topper**. New York: Ballantine/Del Rey, 1980. 208pp. ISBN 0-345-28722-3. (First published by Grosset & Dunlap, 1933). **C**
Sequel: *Topper Takes a Trip*.
Movie version: 1937. Director: Norman McLeod. Stars: Cary Grant, Constance Bennett, and Roland Young. 1979. Director: Charles Dubin. Stars: Kate Jackson, Norman Stevens, and Jack Warden.

George and Marian Kirby, wealthy sophisticates, are surprised to find themselves in a ghostly state. They decide that in order to free themselves from this limbolike existence they must do a good deed. When they decide their mild, henpecked banker, Topper, is a worthy recipient of their attentions, the fun begins. [Ghosts]

382. Snyder, Gene. **Tomb Seven**. New York: Charter, 1985. 279pp. ISBN 0-441-81643-6. **C**

Most archaeological work involves tedious, painstaking searches in out-of-the-way places. Sometimes, however, the scientists find great treasures, making it all seem worthwhile. Tomb Seven, hidden in the mountains of Mexico, would seem to be such a find, but its discoverers have not reckoned with the fury of disturbed ancient gods. [Legends, Aztec]

383. Somtow, S. P. **Vampire Junction**. New York: Berkley, 1985. 362pp. ISBN 0-425-09091-4. (First published by Donning, 1984). **C**

A horrifying and gruesome tale of vampires and rock music. These impressionistic series of images could shatter quiet sleep for some nights to come. [Vampires]

384. Sparger, Rex. **The Bargain**. New York: Bantam, 1983. 152pp. ISBN 0-553-22823-4. (Dark Forces series). **A**

The Coastals, a high school rock group, want success. Little do they realize, though, when they make an agreement with Chort that the deal includes more than fame and fortune. Their very souls are the price they must pay. [The devil]

385. Sparger, Rex. **The Doll**. New York: Bantam, 1983. 135pp. ISBN 0-553-22824-2. (Dark Forces series). **A**

Cassie collects dolls, and when she sees a special, lifelike doll at the state fair, she knows she must have it. But special powers come with the doll, and it has evil designs on Cassie's soul. [Evil]

386. Speare, Elizabeth George. **The Witch of Blackbird Pond**. New York: Laurel-Leaf, 1972. 249pp. ISBN 0-440-49596-2. (First published by Houghton Mifflin, 1958). **A**

Kit Tyler knew her life in cold, colonial Connecticut would be very different from her luxurious home in the Caribbean. She does not realize how very different and dangerous it would be, however, until she is accused of witchcraft. [Witchcraft]

387. Stanwood, Brooks. **The Seventh Child**. New York: Dell, 1982. 315pp. ISBN 0-440-19122-X. **C**
Other works: *The Glow.*

Is it possible for a terrible past to live again? Seven children find out they are merely pawns used by a terrible evil to re-enact a horrible deed from the past. [Witchcraft]

388. Steinbeck, John. **The Acts of King Arthur and His Noble Knights**. New York: Ballantine/Del Rey, 1981. 464pp. ISBN 0-345-28955-2. (First published by Farrar, Straus & Giroux, 1976). **A**
Movie version: *Excalibur:* 1981. Director: John Borman. Stars: Nicol Williamson, Nigel Terry, and Helen Mirren.

A noted American author's version of eight tales from Malory's manuscript about King Arthur and his knights. [Arthurian legends]

389. Stevenson, E. **The Avenging Spirit**. New York: Dell, 1983. 148pp. ISBN 0-440-90001-8. (Twilight series). **A**

Christina is fascinated by the beauty, power, and mystery of the mountain which hovers over Thunder Rock. But her fascination does not bring Christina peace; instead she finds unrest and an increasing sense of doom. [Evil]

390. Stevenson, Robert Louis. **Dr. Jekyll and Mr. Hyde**. New York: Bantam, 1981. 128pp. ISBN 0-553-21200-1. (First published by Longmans, Green, 1888). **D**
Other works: *The Master of Ballantrae; The Supernatural Short Stories of Robert Louis Stevenson.*
Movie versions: 1932. Director: Rouben Mamoulian. Stars: Frederic March and Miriam Hopkins. 1941. Director: Victor Fleming. Stars: Spencer Tracy and Ingrid Bergman.

A respected doctor by day, Dr. Jekyll experiments in his lab and finds a way to alter his appearance and personality to that of dissipated Mr. Hyde, who roams the dark streets of London in search of depraved pleasures. [Science gone wrong]

391.   Stewart, Fred Mustard. **The Mephisto Waltz**. New York: Berkley, 1982. 212pp. ISBN 0-425-05343-1. (First published by Coward-McCann, 1969). **C**
Other works include: *Star Child; A Rage Against Heaven*.
Movie version: 1971. Director: Paul Wendkos. Stars: Alan Alda, Jacqueline Bisset, Barbara Parkins, and Curt Jurgens.

Myles Clarkson, once an aspiring concert pianist, is fascinated by the attention of Duncan Ely, an aging, renowned pianist. Only Myles's wife seems to sense impending doom as Myles becomes more and more manipulated by the sinister Duncan. [Evil]

392.   Stewart, Mary. **The Crystal Cave**. New York: Fawcett/Crest, 1984. 384pp. ISBN 0-449-20644-0. (First published by Morrow, 1970). **C**
Sequels: *The Hollow Hills; The Last Enchantment; The Wicked Day*.

The magical story of Camelot and an early Britain full of magic, as seen through the eyes of Merlin. [Arthurian legends]

393.   Stewart, Mary. **Touch Not the Cat**. New York: Ballantine, 1984. 302pp. ISBN 0-449-20608-4. (First published by Morrow, 1976). **C**

Bryony Ashley must use all of her special powers to solve the mysteries of her family and bring peace to her own life. [Paranormal abilities]

394.   Stewart, Mary. **A Walk in Wolf Wood**. New York: Fawcett/Crest, 1980. 188pp. ISBN 0-449-20111-2. (First published by Morrow, 1980). **B**

John and Margaret follow a strange man into the forest and find themselves in another time. They decide to help Lord Mardian, but quickly discover that evil men do not want Lord Mardian cured of his werewolf curse. [Time travel; Werewolves]

395.   Stewart, Ramona. **Sixth Sense**. New York: Dell, 1980. 211pp. ISBN 0-440-18015-5. (First published by Delacorte, 1979). **A**
Other works: *The Possession of Joel Delaney*.

Nancy Parsons discovers that she has powers of ESP, enabling her to "join" the mind of a vicious killer. Soon, however, the killer finds out about Nancy, and he decides to make her his next victim. [Paranormal abilities]

396.   Stoker, Bram. **Dracula**. New York: Bantam, 1981. 402pp. ISBN 0-553-22148-X. (First published by Constable, 1897). **D**
Other works: *Jewel of the Seven Stars; The Lady of the Shroud; The Lair of the White Worm*.
Movie versions: 1931. Director: Tod Browning. Stars: Bela Lugosi, David Manners, and Helen Chandler. *Count Dracula:* 1970. Director: Jess Frances. Stars: Christopher Lee, Herbert Lom, and Klaus Kinski. 1973. Director: Dan Curtis. Stars: Jack Palance, Simon Ward, Nigel Davenport, and Pamela Brown. 1979. Director: John Badham. Stars: Frank Langella, Laurence Olivier, Donald Pleasence, and Kate Nelligan.

The classic tale which has spawned so many movies, plays, and books. [Vampires]

397. Straub, Peter. **Ghost Story**. New York: Pocket Books, 1979. 567pp. ISBN 0-671-44198-1. (First published by Coward, McCann & Geoghegan, 1978). **C**
Other works: *Floating Dragon; Under Venus;* with Stephen King, *Talisman.*
Movie version: 1981. Director: John Irving. Stars: Fred Astaire, Melvyn Douglas, Douglas Fairbanks, Jr., John Houseman, Craig Wasson, and Alice Krige.

Four old men share a terrible secret from the days of their youth. They think they are safe from repercussions, but they don't reckon on the vengeful spirit of the long-dead girl they once wronged. [Ghosts]

398. Straub, Peter. **Shadowland**. New York: Berkley, 1981. 468pp. ISBN 0-425-05056-4. (First published by Coward, McCann & Geoghegan, 1980). **C**

Two prep school teenagers arrive at Shadowland for a summer vacation. Their vacation, however, turns into a dizzying and mysterious voyage of magic and terror, a vacation from which there may be no escape. [Magic]

399. Streiber, Whitley. **The Hunger**. New York: Pocket Books, 1982. 307pp. ISBN 0-671-42737-7. (First published by William Morrow, 1981). **C**
Other works: *Black Magic; Satan's Church.*
Movie version: 1983. Director: Tony Scott. Stars: Catherine Deneuve, David Bowie, and Susan Sarandon.

Miriam, a true vampire from an ancient race, is forced to outlive all her lovers, who, although they never fully die, are unable to continue forever as her companions. John has been Miriam's lover for 200 years, but his time is drawing to an end, and Miriam must find someone new to take his place. [Vampires]

400. Streiber, Whitley. **The Wolfen**. New York: Bantam, 1979. 275pp. ISBN 0-553-20268-5. (First published by William Morrow, 1978). **C**
Movie version: 1981. Director: Michael Wadleigh. Stars: Albert Finney, Diane Venora, Gregory Hines, and Edward James Olmos.

New York is becoming more and more like a savage jungle every day, in the view of a hardened police detective. Now a new breed of creatures are apparently doing their "work" in the city, causing havoc and death wherever they strike. The beasts are strange, vicious killers, not the creatures usually seen in urban environments. [Monsters]

401. Sutcliff, Rosemary. **The Light beyond the Forest**. London: Knight, 1980. 148pp. ISBN 0-340-25821-7. (First published by Bodley Head, 1979). **A**
Sequels: *The Sword and the Circle; The Road to Camlann.*

This version of the King Arthur legend centers on the quest for the Holy Grail, and how the knights of the round table strive to find this most holy relic. [Arthurian legends]

402. Sykes, Pamela. **Mirror of Danger**. New York: Archway, 1976. 215pp. ISBN 0-671-49518-6. (First published by Thomas Nelson, 1973). **A**

At first it seems like an exciting new game when Lucy meets an old-fashioned girl in the old mirror's reflection. When Alice takes her back in time, however, Lucy realizes that Alice has a frightening purpose to her friendship, one which will keep Lucy trapped in the past forever. [Ghosts]

403. Tannen, Mary. **The Wizard Children of Finn**. New York: Avon/Camelot, 1982. 214pp. ISBN 0-380-57661-9. **B**
      Sequel: *The Lost Legend of Finn.*

When Fiona and her brother, Bran, wander into the wood, they meet a mysterious, enchanted boy named Finn, who takes them to his home—the Ireland of 2,000 years ago. [Time travel]

404. Tarr, Judith. **The Isle of Glass**. New York: TOR, 1986. 276pp. ISBN 0-812-55600-3. (First published by Bluejay, 1985). **A**
      Sequels: *The Hound and the Falcon; The Hounds of God.*

Elf-born Brother Alfred has many trials in the world of humans. His quest to help bring peace to his world seems doomed to failure as he tries to understand the strange ways of mankind. [Fairies; Paranormal abilities]

405. Taylor, Domini. **Gemini**. New York: Fawcett/Crest, 1986. 267pp. ISBN 0-449-21077-4. (First published by Atheneum, 1984). **C**

Peter and Pandora are exceptionally close, even for twins. Alone they have strange powers, but together they possess incredible strength which enables them to do anything they want. [Horror]

406. Tepper, Sheri S. **Blood Heritage**. New York: TOR, 1986. 287pp. ISBN 0-812-52623-6. **C**
      Sequel: *The Bones.*
      Other works: *Jinian Footseer; Marianne, the Magus and the Manticore.*

Badger Ettison misses his wife terribly, but soon discovers that there are worse things in life than death. He finds out that demons are real and the only way he can work his way out of this horrible situation is to resort to magic. [Demons; Horror]

407. Tigges, John. **Evil Dreams**. New York: Leisure, 1986. 397pp. ISBN 0-8439-2309-1. **C**
      Other works: *The Legend of Jean Marie Cardinal.*

Dreams should not have the power to control a person's life, but Jon Ward's dreams of terror are so intense he is desperate to find relief. Then his dreams become even more lifelike, and Jon finds himself overpowered by a vengeful spirit who plans to use Jon for evil purposes. [Demons; Dreams; Horror]

408.   Tigges, John. **Garden of the Incubus**. New York: Leisure, 1982. 319pp. ISBN 0-8439-2371-7. **C**
       Sequels: *Unto the Altar; Kiss Not the Child.*

When Bobbe Moore declares her intention to become a nun rather than marry her handsome suitor, she is almost as surprised as her friends and family. But Bobbe's will does not seem to be her own anymore, and she finds that the convent is not a safe place for her or her soul. [Evil; Possession]

409.   Tolstoy, Alexis. **Vampires: Stories of the Supernatural**. Harmondsworth, England: Penguin, 1946. 183pp. **C**

Scary stories by the cousin of Russian master Leo Tolstoy, including "Amena," "The Family of a Vourdalak," "The Reunion after Three Hundred Years," "The Vampire." [Short stories]

410.   Town, Mary. **Paul's Game**. New York: Laurel-Leaf, 1983. 192pp. ISBN 0-440-96633-7. (First published by Delacorte, 1983). **A**

Andrea and her friend, gentle Julie, have ESP powers. When Paul starts to date Julie it soon becomes plain to Andrea that he is able to influence Julie's behavior and thoughts. It seems that only Andrea will be able to save Julie from Paul's unhealthy influence. [Paranormal abilities]

411.   Trainor, Joseph. **Watery Grave**. New York: Dell, 1983. 168pp. ISBN 0-440-99419-5. (Twilight series). **A**

Something or someone seems to be calling to Julie. Is it Lavinia, whose name appears mysteriously in her schoolbook, or is it the strange man she encounters in the fog while she is trying to find her way home? Whoever it is, there seems to be no escape for Julie. [Ghosts]

412.   Tremayne, Peter. **Bloodright: a Memoir of Mircea, Son of Vlad Tepes, Prince of Wallachia, Also Known as Dracula,... Born on This Earth in the Year of Christ 1431, Who Died in 1476 But Remained Undead ....** New York: Dell, 1980. 251pp. ISBN 0-440-10509-9. (First published as *Dracula Unborn* by Corgi, 1977). **C**
       Sequels: *The Revenge of Dracula; Dracula My Love.*

Mircea lives a swashbuckling life, saving beautiful damsels and defeating evil villains. [Vampires]

413.   Tryon, Thomas. **Harvest Home**. New York: Fawcett, 1978. 415pp. ISBN 0-449-23496-7. (First published by Knopf, 1973). **C**

A peaceful New England town turns from a pleasant home to a haunted, frightening setting for terror and mystery. [Cults; Demons]

414.   Tryon, Thomas. **The Other**. New York: Fawcett/Crest, 1978. 288pp. ISBN 0-449-24088-6. (First published by Knopf, 1971). **C**
       Movie version: 1972. Director: Robert Mulligan. Stars: Uta Hagen, Diana Muldaur, and Chris and Martin Udvarnoky.

How could twins be so different, one so good and one so bad? Only their Russian-born grandmother seems to be aware of what is happening to Niles and Holland. [Evil; Possession]

415. Twain, Mark (pseud. of Samuel Clemens). **A Connecticut Yankee in King Arthur's Court**. New York: Bantam, 1981. 274pp. ISBN 0-553-21143-9. Harmondsworth, England: Penguin, 1972. ISBN 0-14-043064-4. (First published as *Yankee at the Court of King Arthur* by Harper, 1889). **D**
Movie version: 1949. Director: Tay Garnett. Stars: Bing Crosby and Rhonda Fleming.

A practical, hardheaded Yankee goes back in time to King Arthur's court. Unimpressed with magical doings, our hero unveils Merlin as a charlatan and triumphs over evil with plain old American ingenuity. [Arthurian legends; Time travel]

416. Updike, John. **The Witches of Eastwick**. New York: Fawcett/Crest, 1985. 352pp. ISBN 0-449-2064705. (First published by Knopf, 1984). **C**

Suburban women looking for new meaning in life turn to the attractions offered by a fascinating new man in town, who turns out to be the devil himself. [The devil; Witchcraft]

417. Uttley, Alison. **A Traveller in Time**. New York: Ace Fantasy, 1986. 197pp. ISBN 0-441-82213-4. (First published by Faber and Faber, 1939). **A**

Penelope goes to visit relatives who live in an ancient house. There she discovers that she can live in two worlds, the past and the present. In the past world she becomes involved in a dangerous plot to liberate Mary, Queen of Scots. [Time travel]

418. Verne, Jules. **Carpathian Castle**. New York: Ace, 1963. 190pp. (First published in France, 1895). **A**
Other works: *Mysterious Island; 20,000 Leagues Under the Sea.*

The brooding old castle in Transylvania is said to be haunted. An investigation builds to an exciting climax as the stories about the castle are literally and figuratively explored. Not everyone can be convinced, however, that there is a rational explanation for the ghostly occurrences, and even today the castle ruins are the scene of strange and mysterious happenings. [Haunted houses]

419. Vinge, Joan D. **Ladyhawke**. New York: Signet, 1985. 252pp. ISBN 0-451-13321-8. **A**
Movie version: 1985. Director: Richard Donner. Stars: Matthew Broderick, Rutger Hauer, and Michelle Pfeiffer.

The sinister Bishop of Aquila has placed a spell on the woman he wants, beautiful Lady Isabeau, and her lover, Etienne Navarre. By day she is a hawk and by night he is a wolf, together forever, forever apart. Brash Philippe, a young street urchin, is determined to help the doomed and desperate lovers, but finds himself caught up in the bishop's evil schemes. [Black magic; Transformation]

420. Vinge, Joan D. **Santa Claus: The Movie**. New York: Berkley, 1985.
       244pp. ISBN 0-425-08385-3. **A**
       Movie version: 1985. Director: Jeannot Szwarc. Stars: Dudley Moore,
       John Lithgow, David Huddleston, and Burgess Meredith.

Most children stop believing in Santa Claus when they're very young, but
suppose Santa is for real? And what happens if one of his elves decides to
desert Santa's workshop and get involved in the contemporary American
business world? [Legends, Christian]

421. Vonnegut, Kurt. **Slaughterhouse-Five: Or, The Children's Crusade**.
       New York: Dell, 1974. 224pp. ISBN 0-440-18029-5. (First published by
       Delacorte, 1969). **C**
       Movie version: 1972. Director: George Roy Hill. Stars: Ron Sachs, Ron
       Leibman, and Valerie Perrine.

Billy Pilgrim finds himself bounced from one time to another without
logic or will. One moment he may be a student, the next a military prisoner of
war in Dresden, and next an exhibit in a zoo on a faraway planet. [Time travel]

422. Wakefield, H. Russell. **The Best Ghost Stories of H. Russell Wakefield**.
       Chicago: Academy Chicago, 1982. 232pp. ISBN 0-89733-066-8. **C**

Good supernatural stories by an English author, including "The Red
Lodge," " 'He Cometh and He Passeth By'," "Professor Pownall's Over-
sight," "The Seventeenth Hole at Duncaster," " 'Look Up There'," "Blind
Man's Bluff," "Day-Dream in Macedon," "Damp Sheets," "A Black Solitude,"
"The Triumph of Death," "A Kink in Space-Time," "The Gorge of the
Chirels," " 'Immortal Bird'," "Death of a Bumble Bee." [Short stories]

423. Walsh, Jill Paton. **A Chance Child**. New York: Avon, 1978. 139pp.
       ISBN 0-380-48561-1. (First published in the United States by Farrar,
       Straus & Giroux, 1978). **A**

Creep, a desperate abused child, finds himself transported back in time to
a harsh age of child labor. In spite of the hardships, he finds happiness by
means of faith and hard work, leaving a message to be found by those who
search for him. [Time travel]

424. Walter, R. R. **Ladies in Waiting**. New York: TOR, 1986. 411pp. ISBN
       0-812-52700-3. **C**

The old house seems evil to Adrienne as soon as she enters it. There seems
to be spirits all over the house, even in the garden, and their whispers follow
her wherever she goes. Then her husband discovers some portraits of women
hidden from sight, and these women seen to be alive. [Evil; Possession]

425. Walton, Evangeline (pseud. of Evangeline Ensley). **Prince of Annwyn**.
       New York: Ballantine/Del Rey, 1974. 178pp. ISBN 0-345-27737-6.
       (First published by Random House, 1971). **A**
       Sequels: *The Children of Llyr; The Song of Rhiannon; The Island of
       the Mighty*.

The ancient tales of the Mabinogian legend of Wales have served as an inspiration for many writers. Here, the author retells these wonderful stories, including that of Prince Pwyll who is set to a task by the King of Death. Pwyll finds his task complicated by temptation in the form of a beautiful woman, and he fears he may succumb to her charms. [Legends, Celtic; Magic]

426.   Walton, Evangeline (pseud. of Evangeline Ensley). **Witch House**. New York: Ballantine/Del Rey, 1979. 196pp. ISBN 0-345-28020-2. (First published by Arkham House, 1945). **A**

Dr. Gaylord Carew, an investigator of supernatural phenomena, has been called to Witch House in New England by the desperate mother of a child who is overcome by the power and rage of an ancient evil permeating the old house. [Haunted houses]

Ward, Arthur Henry. *See* Rohmer, Sax.

427.   Warner, Sylvia Townsend. **Kingdoms of Elfin**. Harmondsworth, England: Penguin, 1979. 222pp. ISBN 0-1400-4813-8. (First published in the United States by Viking, 1977). **C**

Stories about the complex elfin world and how elves manage to co-exist with humans. The intricacies of the fairy world are explored through the lives and loves of these magical beings who sometimes come to the earth's surface to surprise any human who happens to encounter them. [Fairies]

428.   Warner, Sylvia Townsend. **Lolly Willowes: Or, The Loving Huntsman**. Chicago: Academy Chicago, 1978. 252pp. ISBN 0-915864-92-4. (First published in the United States by Viking, 1926). **C**

A quiet, gentle maiden lady revolts when she is forty-seven and makes a new life for herself. She makes a pact with the devil in order to stop her family from making demands upon her. [The devil; Witchcraft]

429.   Weaver, Lydia. **Splashman**. New York: Signet, 1985. 190pp. ISBN 0-451-14020-6. **A**

Jane and her family find their usual summer fun on the beach destroyed by bad weather and peculiar, strangling seaweed. Then Jane rescues a strange boy, Peter Joyce, who claims his mother was a mermaid. Certainly, there does seem to be something very unusual about Peter. She finds her feelings for him changing from disbelief to sympathy, and finally, to love. [Mermaids]

430.   Wellman, Manly Wade. **The Old Gods Waken**. New York: Berkley, 1984. 192pp. ISBN 0-425-07015-8. (First published by Doubleday, 1979). **C**
Sequels: *After Dark; The Lost and the Lurking; The Hanging Stories.* Other works: *What Dreams May Come; The School of Darkness.*

First of the Silver John novels, the scene is set on Walter Mountain in the peaceful rural south. A strange clash of cultures is due to erupt, however, as two Englishmen, ancient Druids, are determined to arouse the traditional Indian spirits who slumber on the mountain top. Only John seems aware of their plan, and only John is willing to try to stop them. [Legends, Celtic; Legends, Native American]

431. Wells, H. G. **The Invisible Man**. New York: Bantam, 1983. 144pp. ISBN 0-553-21207-9. Bound with *The Time Machine*, New York: Signet, 1982. 320pp. ISBN 0-451-51877-2. (First published in England, 1887). **D**
Other works: *Lost Worlds*.
Movie version: 1933. Director: James Whale. Stars: Claude Rains, Gloria Stuart, and Una O'Connor. 1975. Director: Robert Michael Lewis. Stars: David McCallum, Melinda Fee, and Jackie Cooper.

Many of us have dreamed of the fun it would be if we were invisible, but the adventures of the hapless hero show us that invisibility is really a curse. [Transformation]

432. Wells, H. G. **The Island of Dr. Moreau**. New York: Magnum/Lancer, 1968. 189pp. (First published in England, 1896). **A**
Movie version: 1977. Director: Don Taylor. Stars: Burt Lancaster, Michael York, and Nigel Davenport.

Edward Prendick is rescued from a shipwreck by a mysterious man in a small boat headed for a distant island. When they reach the island, Edward is forced ashore, where he discovers the terrible experiments of the mad Dr. Moreau. [Science gone wrong]

433. Werlin, Marvin, and Mark Werlin. **The Savior**. New York: Dell, 1981. 480pp. ISBN 0-440-17748-0. (First published by Simon & Schuster, 1978). **C**

Christopher McKenzie has special powers, but in using them recklessly he finds he can cause misery and pain to those he loves. [Paranormal abilities]

434. Westall, Robert. **Break of Dark**. Harmondsworth, England: Puffin Plus, 1984. 173pp. ISBN 0-14-031581-0. (First published by Chatto and Windus, 1982). **A**
Other works: *The Haunting of Chas McGee and Other Stories; The Wind Eye*.

Short stories, including "Hitch-hiker," "Blackham's Wimpey," "Fred, Alice and Aunty Lou," "St. Austin Friars," "Sergeant Nice." [Short stories]

435. Westall, Robert. **The Devil on the Road**. New York: Ace, 1985. 200pp. ISBN 0-441-14290-7. (First published by Greenwillow, 1978). **A**

What starts as an aimless summer vacation roaming on a motorbike becomes a strange and desperate quest in another time. Can John Webster save a lovely young witch from death at the hands of dreaded Matthew Hopkins, the Witchfinder General? [Time travel; Witchcraft]

436. Westall, Robert. **The Scarecrows**. Harmondsworth, England: Puffin Plus, 1983. 160pp. ISBN 0-14-031465-2. (First published by Chatto and Windus, 1981). **A**

Simon doesn't like his new stepfather, and he hates the idea of spending the summer at his place in the country. He starts to explore the countryside in order to stay away from home as much as possible, and discovers the old mill house, scene of an old tragedy and full of evil presence. The scarecrows in the nearby field are odd and also full of evil. Simon begins to feel trapped, and he doesn't know where to go for help. [Evil]

437. Westall, Robert. **The Watch House**. Harmondsworth, England: Puffin Plus, 1980. 204pp. ISBN 0-14-031285-4. (First published by Macmillan, 1977). **A**

Anne, deserted by her father and unwanted by her mother, is sent to live with an old servant in a house next to a desolate old watch house. Lonely and unhappy, Anne starts to explore her new home and finds in the old watch house an evil presence that soon makes itself known to her. [Ghosts]

438. Wheatley, Dennis. **The Devil Rides Out**. London: Arrow, 1974. 320pp. ISBN 0-0990-7240-8. (First published by Hutchinson, 1956). **C**
Other works: *The Haunting of Toby Jugg; The Ka of Gifford Hillary; The Gateway to Hell; The Satanist.*

Simon Aron seems to be in trouble, and his friends, the Duc de Richleau, Rex van Ryn, and Richard Eaton, decide to investigate. What they discover is a vile satanic plot, one which threatens to destroy all of them, including the beautiful young woman who is slated to be a human sacrifice. [Satanism]

439. Wheatley, Dennis. **The Irish Witch**. London: Arrow, 1975. 446pp. ISBN 0-09-910440-7. (First published by Hutchinson, 1973). **C**

The early years of the nineteenth century were turbulent times in England and Ireland. Roger Brook, a government agent deeply involved in the complex dealings of Napoleonic politics and war, finds to his dismay that his beloved son has joined a revival of the notorious satanic cult, the Hellfire Club. [Satanism]

440. Wheatley, Dennis. **Strange Conflict**. New York: Ballantine, 1972. 320pp. SBN 345-02988-7-150. (First published by Hutchinson, 1941). **C**

Nazi use of occult secrets has been written about before, as has the theme of good and evil. Wheatley's protagonists, a wise French duke, a sturdy American, and a brave English Jew, pit their skills against the Nazi villains. The climax of the book is set in Haiti where voodoo rites blend with adventures on the astral plane. Good triumphs, of course, in the end, leaving our heroes ready to take on further occult adventures. [Black magic; Voodoo]

441. Wheatley, Dennis. **To the Devil — A Daughter**. New York: Bantam, 1968. 329pp. (First published by Hutchinson, 1953). **C**
Movie version: 1976. Director: Peter Sykes. Stars: Richard Widmark, Christopher Lee, Honor Blackman, and Nastassia Kinski.

A beautiful young woman has been promised to the devil in order to give her father good fortune. As her twenty-first birthday approaches (the date she has been promised for the sacrifice), her father attempts to hide her. Well-meaning neighbor, Molly Fountain, uncovers these evil goings-on and joins in the effort to save Christina from her fate. [The devil; Satanism]

442. White, T. H. **The Once and Future King**. New York: Berkley, 1983. 640pp. ISBN 0-425-06310-0. (First published by Putnam, 1958). **A**
Sequel: *The Book of Merlin.*
Other works: *Mistress Masham's Respose.*

Used as the basis for Disney's animated feature, *The Sword and the Stone*, this version of King Arthur's story is told with humor and style from the viewpoint of the insecure young king, or Wart. [Arthurian legends]

443. Whitney, Phyllis A. **Mystery of the Mysterious Traveler**. New York: Signet/New American, 1974. 172pp. ISBN 0-451-09847-1. (First published as *The Island of the Dark Woods* by Westminister, 1967). **C**

Laurie is excited, much more excited than her sister Celia, about their visit to Aunt Serena. When she sees the huge, gloomy house on Staten Island, she suspects there's some kind of mystery going on. This is confirmed when she encounters the phantom stagecoach. [Ghosts]

444. Whitten, Les. **The Alchemist**. New York: Zebra, 1986. 412pp. ISBN 0-8217-1865-7. (First published by Charterhouse, 1973). **C**

Martin Dobecker seems to be a quiet, placid sort of fellow, quite satisfied with his routine life. Little did people know, however, that he had a most peculiar hobby, that of experimenting with black magic. [Alchemy; Black magic]

445. Wilde, Oscar. **The Picture of Dorian Gray**. New York: Laurel-Leaf, 1956. 224pp. ISBN 0-440-36914-2. (First published by Ward Lock, 1891). **D**
Movie version: 1945. Director: Albert Lewin. Stars: George Saunders, Donna Reed, and Angela Lansbury.

Eternal youth is granted to Dorian Gray, who remains youthful in appearance while his portrait grows old and haggard. Gray's life of dissipation seems to have no checks and controls, but he finds that even those who possess a charmed life must eventually pay the price. [Eternal life]

446. Willard, Nancy. **Things Invisible to See**. New York: Bantam, 1986. 262pp. ISBN 0-553-25563-0. (First published by Knopf, 1985). **C**

Ben Harkissian loves baseball. Little does he realize that the day will come when he must play his team against one drafted by death, who has all the dead baseball greats on his side. [Heaven]

447. Williams, Charles. **Many Dimensions**. Grand Rapids, Mich.: Eerd-
mans, 1981. 269pp. ISBN 0-802-281221-X. (First published by Victor
Gollancz, 1931). **C**
Other works: *All Hallows' Eve; Descent into Hell; The Place of the
Lion; War in Heaven; The Greater Trumps.*

A scientist is able to travel through time by use of a mysterious and
ancient stone. [Legends, Christian; Time travel]

448. Williamson, J. N. **Premonition**. New York: Leisure, 1981. 287pp. ISBN
0-8439-0959-5. **C**
Other works: *The Houngan; The Tulpa; The Ritual; Death Coach;
Death-Angel; The Offspring; The Evil One; Playmates; Ghost Mansion; Ladies of the Longest Night.*

Ingrid Solomon is a beautiful woman, but one beset by frightening
secrets. She is obsessed by the notion of eternal life and is dabbling in scientific
experiments which might help her dream come true. She has not reckoned with
other powers, however, powers which will punish her for trying to discover
arcane mysteries. [Magic; Science gone wrong]

449. Wilson, Colin. **The Schoolgirl Murder Case**. Chicago: Academy
Chicago, 1982. 255pp. ISBN 0-586-04232-6. (First published by Hart-
Davis, 1974). **C**
Other works: *Labyrinth.*

The murder of a prostitute dressed like a schoolgirl leads Saltfleet of
Scotland Yard into a world of occult, evil and mysterious activity. [Satanism]

450. Wilson, F. Paul. **The Keep**. New York: Berkley, 1982. 406pp. ISBN
0-425-05324-5. (First published by William Morrow, 1981). **C**
Other works: *The Touch.*
Movie version: 1983. Director: Michael Mann. Stars: Scott Glenn, Ian
McKellan, and Alberta Watson.

The awesome castle deep in the Carpathian Mountains is covered with
mysterious symbols and shrouded in secrets. The Nazis cannot cope with the
savage murders of their soldiers. A learned professor and his beautiful daughter
are summoned to unravel the mystery, and they discover the original
evil—Rasalom, a monster who feeds on human despair and misery. [Monsters;
Vampires]

451. Wilson, F. Paul. **The Tomb**. New York: Berkley, 1984. 404pp. ISBN
0-425-07295-9. (First published by Whispers Press, 1984). **C**

Repairman Jack is a fixer, not of broken appliances as his father thinks,
but of misjustice. Jack can be hired to right wrongs, according to his morals.
One day he takes two unusual, and he thinks unconnected, jobs which lead
him into a horrifying fight to save a child from the terror of sacrifice to Kali,
the rapacious Indian goddess of destruction. [Legends, Indian; Monsters]

452.   Windsor, Patricia. **Killing Time**. New York: Laurel-Leaf, 1983. 188pp. ISBN 0-440-94471-6. (First published by Harper & Row, 1980). **A**

After his parents' divorce, Sam is dragged to the country. Life in the sticks isn't as dull as Sam thinks at first, especially when he finds Druid worshippers up to no good. [Cults; Legends, Celtic]

453.   Winston, Daoma. **A Sweet Familiarity**. New York: Critic's Choice, 1986. 254pp. ISBN 1-55547-111-0. (First published by Interpub Communications, 1981). **C**

Like many small towns, Meadowville has always had a few families of power. In this instance, the two families, the Vickerys and the Paiges, were friends for many years until a tragedy occurred. Maggie is dead now, but when Claude, who had loved her years ago, returns to Meadowville, Maggie's spirit is ready for revenge. [Ghosts]

454.   Woolrich, Cornell. **Vampire's Honeymoon**. New York: Carroll & Graf, 1985. 223pp. ISBN 0-88184-132-3. **C**

Four stories about vampires by the author of *Rear Window* include "Vampire's Honeymoon;" "Graves for the Dead;" "I'm Dangerous Tonight;" "The Street of Jungle Death." [Short stories; Vampires]

455.   Worth, Valerie. **Gypsy Gold**. New York: Farrar, Straus & Giroux, 1986. 176pp. ISBN 0-374-42820-4. (First published by Farrar, Straus & Giroux, 1983). **A**
       Other works: *Curlicues; Fox Hill.*

When young Miranda's parents decide that her future must be that of wife to an elderly, wealthy man, she revolts and runs away with the gypsies. There she discovers that fortune-telling is more than a con game. She also finds out new truths about herself. [Gypsy lore]

456.   Wright, Betty Ren. **Ghosts Beneath Our Feet**. New York: Scholastic, 1984. 137pp. ISBN 0-590-33704-1. **B**
       Other works: *Secret Windows.*

Katie, her mother, and stepbrother are spending the summer in a desolate old mining town in upper Michigan. One of Katie's new friends tells her stories about the trapped ghosts of miners who died years before. Are they truly trying to escape? And who is the strange, shadowy ghost girl who seems to be trying to tell Katie something? [Ghosts]

457.   Wright, T. M. **A Manhattan Ghost Story**. New York: TOR, 1984. 381pp. ISBN 0-812-52750-X. **C**
       Sequel: *The Waiting Room.*
       Other works: *Carlisle Street; The People of the Dark; The Woman Next Door; The Children of the Island; The Playground.*

Ghosts don't always look transparent and dress in trailing white draperies. Some seem as normal as other people, especially when the setting is New York City. [Ghosts]

458. Wrightson, Patricia. **The Ice Is Coming**. New York: Ballantine/Del Rey, 1981. 196pp. ISBN 0-345-33248-2. (First published in the United States by Atheneum, 1977). **A**
Sequels: *The Bright Dark Water; Journey Behind the Wind.*

Wirrum, a young aborigine in Australia, senses that something is wrong with the land. Frost and ice have begun forming during the hottest summer months, and there seems to be a restlessness about the elusive spirits of the countryside. Then he discovers that the Ninya, the ancient ice-spirits, are loose and must be brought back under control, or the country will become shrouded with a never-ending winter. [Legends, Aboriginal]

459. Wynne Jones, Diana. **Fire and Hemlock**. New York: Berkley, 1985. 280pp. ISBN 0-425-09504-5. (First published by Greenwillow, 1984). **A**
Other works: *Witch Week; The Homeward Bounders; The Magicians of Caprona; Charmed Life; Power of Three.*

Polly, a casual young college student, finds herself with muddled memories and odd thoughts about the past. She's not sure what is real and what she may have read in her beloved fantasy books. Soon it becomes very confused as Polly struggles with her dreams of the past. Her own actions somehow seem to be the key for learning what has truly happened. [Altered states of consciousness]

460. Yarbro, Chelsea Quinn. **Hotel Transylvania**. New York: Signet, 1979. 279pp. ISBN 0-451-08461-6. (First published by St. Martin's, 1978). **C**
Sequels: *The Palace; Blood Games; Path of the Eclipse; Tempting Fate; The Saint-Germaine Chronicles.*
Other works: *Cautionary Tales; Dead & Buried; False Dawn; Aristo; The Godforsaken.*

Beautiful young women sometimes fall in love with fascinating older men. Madeleine, however, makes the mistake of falling in love with a vampire, who fortunately helps to save her from others more evil than himself. [Vampires]

461. Yarbro, Chelsea Quinn. **A Mortal Glamour**. New York: Bantam, 1985. 308pp. ISBN 0-553-245887-2. **C**

Strange, frightening things are happening in the fourteenth century convent at Avignon. The gentle nuns seem tempted beyond belief as they are courted by a fascinating emissary of the devil who is determined to collect souls for his master. [The devil; Evil]

462. Yolen, Jane. **Merline's Booke**. New York: Ace, 1986. 176pp. ISBN 0-441-52552-0. **C**
Other works: *Cards of Grief; Dragonfield and Other Stories; The Magic Three of Salatia.*

The land of Camelot is a magical one, full of dragons, magic, and sorcerers. The most powerful sorcerer of all is Merlin, a wizard of skill and yet susceptible to human foibles. [Arthurian legends]

463.   York, Carol B. **On That Dark Night**. New York: Bantam, 1985. 128pp. ISBN 0-553-25207-0. **A**
Other works: *I Will Make You Disappear; The Ghost of the Isherwoods.*

Allison Morley is determined to find out about the things that are frightening her friend Julie. Can Julie really be possessed by someone who lived eighty years ago? Allison's and Julie's search becomes a terrifying journey into a frightening past. [Reincarnation]

Part 2
Anthologies

464. Asimov, Isaac, Martin H. Greenberg, and Charles G. Waugh, eds. **Young Monsters**. New York: Harper & Row, 1985. 213pp. ISBN 0-06-020169-X. **B**
Other works compiled by editors: *Young Ghosts*.

A collection of stories about some disgusting youngsters, all monsters, including "Homecoming" (Ray Bradbury); "Good-by, Miss Patterson" (Phyllis MacLennan); "Disturb Not My Slumbering Fair" (Chelsea Quinn Yarbro); "The Wheelbarrow Boy" (Richard Parker); "The Cabbage Patch" (Theodore R. Cogswell); "The Thing Waiting Outside" (Barbara Williamson); "Red as Blood" (Tanith Lee); "Gabriel-Ernest" (Saki); "Fritzchen" (Charles Beaumont); "The Young One" (Jerome Bixby); "Optical Illusion" (Mack Reynolds); "Idiot's Crusade" (Clifford D. Simak); "One for the Road" (Stephen King); "Angelica" (Jane Yolen). [Monsters; Short stories]

465. Bleiler, Everett F., ed. **A Treasury of Victorian Ghost Stories**. New York: Scribner's, 1983. 358pp. ISBN 0-684-17823-0. **C**

A selection of tales by a noted expert on Gothic literature includes "To Be Read at Dusk" (Charles Dickens); "The Ghost in the Bride's Chamber" (Charles Dickens); "Nine O'Clock!" (Wilkie Collins); "The Dutch Officer's Story" (Mrs. Catherine Crowe); "Wicked Captain Walshawe, of Wauling" (J. S. Le Fanu); "A Curious Experience" (Mrs. Henry Wood); "Le Vert Galant the Nose" (Rhoda Broughton); "Ken's Mystery" (Julian Hawthorne); "A Terrible Vengeance" (Mrs. J. H. Riddell); "The Old Lady in Black" (Anonymous); "The Library Window" (Mrs. Margaret Oliphant); "The Empty Picture Frame" (Mrs. Alfred Baldwin); "A Grammatical Ghost" (Elia W. Peattie); "The Mystery of the Semi-Detached" (E. Nesbit); "My Enemy and Myself" (Vincent O'Sullivan); "Midday Magic" (Paul Heyse); "Witch In-Grain" (R. Murray Gilchrist); "A Stray Reveler" (Emma Dawson); "The Vanishing House" (Bernard Capes); "Bodies of the Dead" (Ambrose Bierce); "Death and the Woman" (Gertrude Atherton); "The Laird's Luck" (Arthur Quiller-Couch). [Ghosts; Short stories]

466. Campbell, Ramsey, ed. **New Terrors II**. New York: Pocket Books, 1984. 256pp. ISBN 0-671-45117-0. (First published by Pan Books, 1980). **C**

Grisly little stories to make you shiver and scream, including "Sun City" (Lisa Tuttle); "Time to Laugh" (Joan Aiken); "Bridal Suite" (Graham Masterton); "The Miraculous Cairn" (Christopher Priest); "The Rubber Room" (Robert Bloch); "Drama in Five Acts" (Giles Gordon); "The Initiation" (Jack Sullivan); "Lucille Would Have Known" (John Burke); "The Funny Face Murders" (R. A. Lafferty); "Femme Fatale" (Marianne Leconte); "Can You Still See Me?" (Margaret Dickson); "One Way Out" (Felice Picano); "The Ice Monkey" (M. John Harrison); "Symbiote" (andrew j. offutt); "Across the Water to Skye" (Charles L. Grant). [Horror; Short stories]

467. Cerf, Bennett, ed. **Famous Ghost Stories**. New York: Random/ Vintage, 1956. 361pp. ISBN 0-394-70140-2. **C**

Some classic tales collected by a noted anthologist, including "The Haunted and the Haunters" (Edward Bulwer-Lytton); "The Damned Thing" (Ambrose Bierce); "The Monkey's Paw" (W. W. Jacobs); "The Phantom Ricksaw" (Rudyard Kipling); "The Willows" (Algernon Blackwood); "The Rival Ghosts" (Branden Matthews); "The Man Who Went Too Far" (E. F. Benson); "The Mezzotint" (Montague Rhodes James); "The Open Window" (Saki); "The Beckoning Fair One" (Oliver Onions); "On the Brighton Road" (Richard Middleton); "The Considerate Hosts" (Thorp McClusky); "August Heat" (W. F. Harvey); "The Return of Andrew Bentley" (August Derleth and Mark Schorer); "The Supper at Elsinor" (Isak Dinesen); "The Current Crop of Ghost Stories" (Bennett Cerf). [Ghosts; Short stories]

468. Child, Lincoln, ed. **Dark Company: The Ten Greatest Ghost Stories**. New York: St. Martin's, 1984, 356pp. ISBN 0-312-18232-5. (First published by St. Martin's, 1983). **C**

One collector's selection of the ten best, which include "Fall of the House of Usher" (Edgar Allan Poe); "Jolly Corner" (Henry James); "Green Tea" (Sheridan Le Fanu); "The Mezzotint" (M. R. James); "The Great God Pan" (Arthur Machen); "The Willows" (Algernon Blackwood); "The Shadow Out of Time" (H. P. Lovecraft). [Ghosts; Short stories]

469. Cuddon, J. A., ed. **The Penguin Book of Ghost Stories**. Harmondsworth, England: Penguin, 1985. 512pp. ISBN 0-14-006800-7. **C**

Some delightfully scary stories, both old and new, including "The Beggarwoman of Locarno" (Heinrich von Kleist); "The Entail" (E. T. A. Hoffman); "Wandering Willie's Tale" (Walter Scott); "The Queen of Spades" (Alexander Pushkin); "The Old Nurse's Story" (Elizabeth Gaskell); "The Open Door" (Margaret Oliphant); "Mr. Justice Harbottle" (Sheridan Le Fanu); "Le Horla" (Guy de Maupassant); "Sir Edmund Orme" (Henry James); "Angeline, or the Haunted House" (Emile Zola); "The Moonlit Road" (Ambrose Bierce); "A Haunted Island" (Algernon Blackwood); "The Rose Garden" (M. R. James); "The Return of Imray" (Rudyard Kipling); "My Adventure in Norwalk" (A. J. Alan); "The Inexperienced Ghost" (H. G. Wells); "The Room in the Tower" (E. F. Benson); "One Who Saw" (A. M. Burrage); "Afterward" (Edith Wharton); "The Wardrobe" (Thomas Mann); "The Buick Saloon" (Ann Bridge); "The Tower" (Marghanita Laski); "Footsteps in the Snow" (Mario Soldati); "The Wind" (Ray Bradbury); "Exorcizing Baldassare" (Edward Hyams); "The

Leaf-Sweeper" (Muriel Spark); " 'Dear Ghost ...' " (Fielden Hughes); "Sonata for Harp and Bicycle" (Joan Aiken); "Come and Get Me" (Elizabeth Walter); "Andrina" (George MacKay Brown); "The Axe" (Penelope Fitzgerald); "The Game of Dice" (Alain Danielou); "The July Ghost" (A. S. Byatt). [Ghosts; Short stories]

470. Cuddon, J. A., ed. **The Penguin Book of Horror Stories**. Harmondsworth, England: Penguin, 1984. 607pp. ISBN 0-14-006799-X. C

This collection of fine tales of shivery horror includes "The Monk of Horror, or The Conclave of Corpses" (Anonymous); "The Astrologer's Prediction, or The Maniac's Fate" (Anonymous); "The Expedition to Hell" (James Hogg); "Mateo Falcone" (Prosper Merimee); "The Case of M. Valdemar" (Edgar Allan Poe); "La Grande Breteche" (Honore de Balzac); "The Romance of Certain Old Clothes" (Henry James); "Who Knows?" (Guy de Maupassant); "The Body Snatcher (Robert Louis Stevenson); "The Death of Olivier Becaille" (Emile Zola); "The Boarded Window" (Ambrose Bierce); "Lost Hearts" (M. R. James); "The Sea-Raiders" (H. G. Wells); "The Derelict" (William Hope Hodgson); "Thurnley Abbey" (Perceval Landon); "The Fourth Man" (James Russell); "In the Penal Colony" (Franz Kafka); "The Waxwork" (A. M. Burrage); "Mrs. Amworth" (E. F. Benson); "The Reptile" (Augustus Muir); "Mr. Meldrum's Mania" (John Metcalfe); "The Beast with Five Fingers" (William Fryer Harvey); "Dry September" (William Faulkner); "Crouching at the Door" (D. K. Broster); "The Two Bottles of Relish" (Lord Dunsany); "The Man Who Liked Dickens" (Evelyn Waugh); "Taboo" (Geoffrey Household); "The Thought" (L. P. Hartley); "Comrade Death" (Gerald Kersh); "Leningen Versus the Ants" (Carl Stephenson); "The Brink of Darkness" (Yvor Winters); "Activity Time" (Monica Dickens); "Earth to Earth" (Robert Graves); "The Dwarf" (Ray Bradbury); "The Portobello Road" (Muriel Spark); "No Flies on Frank" (John Lennon); "Sister Coxall's Revenge" (Dawn Muscillo); "Thou Shalt Not Suffer a Witch ..." (Dorothy K. Haynes); "The Terrapin" (Patricia Highsmith); "Man from the South" (Roald Dahl); "Uneasy Homecoming" (Will F. Jenkins); "The Squarist" (J. N. Allan); "An Interview with M. Chakko" (Vilas Sarang). [Horror; Short stories]

471. Danby, Mary, ed. **The [numbered] Armada Ghost Book**. London: Armada/Fontana, 197?- . (Books 1-13 in the series edited by Christine Bernard and Mary Danby). B

Primarily English stories for younger teens. Stories in book 14 include "The Longest Journey" (Catherine Gleason); "The Junk Room" (Terry Tapp); "Under the Bedclothes" (David Langford); "Gibson's" (Ann Pilling); "The Ghost of Smeaton Hall" (Geoffrey Palmer and Noel Lloyd); "The Third Eye" (R. Chetwynd-Hayes); "In Flanders Fields" (Frances Thomas); "Can't Help Laughing" (Alison Prince); "The Train Watchers" (Sydney J. Bounds); "The Ghost Writer" (Mary Danby).

Book 15, published in 1983, includes "Run for Your Life" (Philip Sidney Jennings); "Hallowe'en" (Rita Morris); "Who's a Pretty Boy, Then?" (Jan Mark); "The Patchwork Quilt" (August Derleth); "The Sound of Sirens" (Tony Richards); "Spirit of the Trail" (Sydney J. Bounds); "Christmas in the

Rectory" (Catherine Storr); "The Servant" (Alison Prince); "Whoever Heard of a Haunted Lift?" (Alan W. Lear); "Mr. Jones" (Mary Danby). [Ghosts; Short stories]

472. Danby, Mary, ed. **Nightmares**. London: Armada, 1983- . **A**

Longer stories which build to nice, scary endings. Contents of *Nightmares 3* include "Clifftops" (Antony Bennett); "Barnacles" (Johnny Yen); "Dead Letter" (Alan W. Lear); "House of Horror" (Sydney J. Bounds); "The Diary" (Samantha Lee); "Shadow of the Rope" (Roger Malisson); "Joplin's" (Brian Mooney); "The Shaft" (Philip C. Heath); "Old Wiggie" (Mary Danby). [Horror; Short stories]

473. Dann, Jack, and Gardner Dozois, eds. **Mermaids!** New York: Ace Fantasy, 1986. 260pp. ISBN 0-441-52567-9. **C**

Other collections by the same editors: *Magicats!; Sorcerors!; Bestiary!*

Stories about mythical creatures of the sea include "Nothing in the Rules" (L. Sprague de Camp); "She Sells Sea Shells" (Paul Darcy Boles); "The Soul Cages" (T. Crofton Croker); "Sweetly the Waves Call to Me" (Pat Murphy); "Driftglass" (Samuel R. Delany); "Mrs. Pigafetta Swims Wells" (Reginald Bretnor); "The Nebraskan and the Nereid" (Gene Wolfe); "The Lady and the Merman" (Jane Yolen); "The White Seal Maid" (Jane Yolen); "The Fisherman's Wife" (Jane Yolen); "Till Human Voices Wake Us" (Lewis Shiner); "A Touch of Strange" (Theodore Sturgeon); "Something Rich and Strange" (Randall Garrett and Avram Davidson); "The Crest of Thirty-Six" (Davis Grubb); "The Shannon Merrow" (Cooper McLaughlin); "Fish Story" (Leslie Charteris); "In the Islands" (Pat Murphy). [Mermaids; Short stories]

474. Dann, Jack, and Gardner Dozois, eds. **Unicorns!** New York: Ace Fantasy, 1982. 308pp. ISBN 0-441-85444-3. **C**

A collection of sixteen magical tales about a beloved, mythical beast, the unicorn, including "The Spoor of the Unicorn" (Avram Davidson); "The Silken Swift" (Theodore Sturgeon); "Eudoric's Unicorn" (L. Sprague de Camp); "The Flight of the Horse" (Larry Niven); "On the Downhill Side" (Harlan Ellison); "The Night of the Unicorn" (Thomas Burnett Swamm); "Mythological Beast" (Stephen R. Donaldson); "The Final Quarry" (Eric Norden); "Elfleda" (Vonda N. McIntyre); "The White Donkey" (Ursula K. Le Guin); "Unicorn Variation" (Roger Zelazny); "The Sacrifice" (Gardner Dozois); "The Unicorn" (Frank Owen); "The Woman the Unicorn Loved" (Gene Wolfe); "The Forsaken" (Bev Evans); "The Unicorn" (T. H. White). [Unicorns; Short stories]

475. Furman, A. L., ed. **Ghost Stories**. New York: Archway, 1964. 163pp. ISBN 0-671-52525-5. (First published as *Teen-Age Ghost Stories* by Simon & Schuster, 1961). **A**

Good ghost stories for teen readers, including "Ghost Alarm" (Carl Henry Rathjen); "Ghost of Black John" (William MacKellar); "Dark Flowers" (Kay Hangaard); "The Ghost of Old Stone Fort" (Harry Harrison Kroll); "Valley of No Return" (Willis Lindquist); "Mystery of the Ghost Junk" (James Benedict Moore); "The Haunted Pavilion" (Patricia McCune); "The Haunted Tumbler" (Diana Meyers). [Ghosts; Short stories]

476. Grant, Charles L., ed. **Nightmares**. New York: Berkley, 1984. 224pp. ISBN 0-425-05955-3. (First published by Playboy, 1979). **C** Other compilations: *Fears; A Glow of Candles and Other Stories; Horrors; Midnight.*

This acknowledged expert on horror is considered to be one of the best anthologists working today. His collection includes "Suffer the Little Children" (Stephen King), "Peekaboo" (Bill Pronzini), "Daughter of the Golden West" (Dennis Etchison), "The Duppy Tree" (Steven Edward McDonald), "Naples" (Avram Davidson), "Seat Partner" (Chelsea Quinn Yarbro), "Camps" (Jack Dann), "The Anchoress" (Beverly Evans), "Transfer" (Barry N. Malzberg), "Unknown Drives" (Richard Christian Matheson), "The Night of the Piasa" (George W. Proctor and J. C. Green), "The Runaway Lovers" (Ray Russell), "Fisherman's Log" (Peter D. Pautz), "I Can't Help Saying Goodbye" (Ann MacKenzie), "Midnight Hobo" (Ramsey Campbell), "Snakes and Snails" (Jack C. Haldeman II), "Mass without Voices" (Arthur L. Samuels), "He Kilt It with a Stick" (William F. Nolan), "The Ghouls" (R. Chetwynd-Hayes). [Horror; Short stories]

477. Grant, Charles L., ed. **Shadows**. (Numbered series 1-) New York: Berkley, 1983- . (First published by Doubleday, 1982). **C**

A fine continuing series of stories by leading contemporary writers of horror. Contents of volume 5 include "Introduction" (Charles L. Grant), "The Gorgon" (Tanith Lee), "Stone Head" (Steve Rasnic Tem), "Pieta" (Alan Ryan), "Boxes" (Al Sarrantonio), "And I'll Be with You By and By" (Avon Swofford), "Dark Wings" (Phyllis Eisenstein), "Estrella" (Terry L. Parkinson), "Singles" (Marta Randall), "The Piano Man" (Beverly Evans), "Following the Way" (Alan Ryan), "Renewal" (Chelsea Quinn Yarbro). [Horror; Short stories]

478. Green, Roger Lancelyn, ed. **A Book of Dragons**. Harmondsworth, England: Puffin, 1973. 250pp. ISBN 0-14-03-0606-4. (First published by Hamish Hamilton, 1970). **A**

Stories and poems about dragons, arranged in four sections: "Dragons of Ancient Days," "Dragons of the Dark Ages," "Dragons of Folklore," and "Dragons of Later Days." Stories include "Jason and the Dragon of Colchis," "The Song of Orpheus" (Andrew Lang, translator), "The Boy and the Dragon," "The Dragon of Macedon," "The Fox and the Dragon," "The Dragon and the Peasant," "The Dragon's Egg," "Dragons and Elephants," "Sigurd the Dragon-Slayer," "Beowolf and the Dragon," "Ragnar Shaggy-Legs and the Dragons," "An Adventure of Digenes the Borderer," "The Red Dragon of Wales," "Sir Tristram in Ireland," "Sir Lancelot and the Dragon" (Sir Thomas Malory), "St. George and the Dragon," "The Mummers' Play," "Sir John Maundeville's Dragon" (Jean D'Outremeuse), "The Dragons of Rhodes, Lucerne, and Somerset," "The Laidly Worm" (Joseph Jacobs), "The Lambton Worm" (Joseph Jacobs), "The Little Bull-Calf" (Joseph Jacobs), "The Dragon and His Grandmother" (Mary Sellar), "The Dragon of the North," "The Master Thief and the Dragon," "Stam Bolovan and the Dragon," "The Prince and the Dragon," "The Cock and the Dragon," "The Chinese Dragons," "The Red Cross Knight and the Dragon" (Edmund Spenser), "The

Shepherd of the Giant Mountains" (M. B. Smedley after Fouque), "Jabber-wocky" (Lewis Carroll), "The Lady Dragonissa" (Andrew Lang), "The Fiery Dragon" (E. Nesbit), "The Dragon at Hide-and-Seek" (G. K. Chesterton), "Conrad and the Dragon" (L. P. Hartley), "The Hoard" (J. R. R. Tolkien), "The Dragon Speaks" (C. S. Lewis), "Epilogue" (St. John the Divine). [Dragons; Short stories]

479. Greenberg, Martin Harry, Richard Matheson, and Charles G. Waugh, eds. **The Twilight Zone: The Original Stories**. New York: Avon, 1985. 550pp. ISBN 0-380-89601-X. **C**
Movie version: see item 360.

Tales from the popular television series written by authors other than Rod Serling (see item 360), including "Preface" (Carol Serling), "Introduction" (Richard Matheson), "One for the Angels" (Anne Serling-Sutton), "Perchance to Dream" (Charles Beaumont), "Disappearing Act" (Richard Matheson), "Time Enough at Last" (Lynn A. Venable), "What You Need" (Lewis Padgett), "Third from the Sun" (Richard Matheson), "Elegy" (Charles Beaumont), "It's a *Good* Life" (Jerome Bixby), "The Valley Was Still" (Manly Wade Wellman), "The Jungle" (Charles Beaumont), "To Serve Man" (Damon Knight), "Little Girl Lost" (Richard Matheson), "Four O'Clock" (Price Day), "I Sing the Body Electric!" (Ray Bradbury), "The Changing of the Guard" (Anne Serling-Sutton), "In Him Image" (Charles Beaumont), "Mute" (Richard Matheson), "Death Ship" (Richard Matheson), "The Devil, You Say?" (Charles Beaumont), "Steel" (Richard Matheson), "Nightmare at 20,000 Feet" (Richard Matheson), "The Old Man" (Henry Slesar), "The Self-Improvement of Salvadore Ross" (Henry Slesar), "The Beautiful People" (Charles Beaumont), "Long Distance Call" (Richard Matheson), "An Occurrence at Owl Creek Bridge" (Ambrose Bierce). [Short stories]

480. Haining, Peter, ed. **The Ghost's Companion: Stories of the Super-natural**. Harmondsworth, England: Puffin, 1978. 222pp. (First published by Victor Gollancz, 1975). **A**

An occult researcher and writer's collection, which includes "A School Story" (M. R. James), "The Red Lodge" (H. R. Wakefield), "The Furnished Room" (O. Henry), "A Haunted Island" (Algernon Blackwood), "My Own True Ghost Story" (Rudyard Kipling), "The Boy who Drew Cats" (Lafcadio Hearn), "The Monstrance" (Arthur Machen), "Escort" (Daphne de Maurier), "South Sea Bubble" (Hammond Innes), "Hallowe'en for Mr. Faulkner" (August Derleth), "The Ghost" (Richard Hughes), "The Case of the Red-Headed Women" (Dennis Wheatley), "Smoke Ghost" (Fritz Leiber), "Aunt Jezebel's House" (Joan Aiken), "Fever Dream" (Ray Bradbury). [Ghosts; Short stories]

481. Haining, Peter, ed. **The Lucifer Society: Macabre Tales by Great Modern Writers**. New York: Signet, 1973. 256pp. (First published by Taplinger, 1972). **C**

Terrifying stories about strange happenings of a supernatural nature, in-cluding "Man Overboard" (Sir Winston Churchill), "Timber" (John Gals-worthy), "The Angry Street" (G. K. Chesterton), "The Call of Wings" (Agatha

Christie), "The Cherries" (Lawrence Durrell), "A Man from Glasgow" (Somerset Maugham), "Earth to Earth" (Robert Graves), "The Grey Ones" (J. B. Priestley), "The Man Who Didn't Ask Why" (C. S. Forester), "All but Empty" (Graham Greene), "Animals or Human Beings" (Angus Wilson), "Something Strange" (Kingsley Amis), "The Post-Mortem Murder" (Sinclair Lewis), "The Dance" (F. Scott Fitzgerald), "A Rose for Emily" (William Faulkner), "The Bronze Door" (Raymond Chandler), "A Man Who Had No Eyes" (MacKinlay Kantor), "The Affair at 7 Rue de M---" (John Steinbeck), "The Snail Watcher" (Patricia Highsmith), "Inferiority Complex" (Evan Hunter), "The Terrible Answer" (Paul Gallico), "Miriam" (Truman Capote), "Exterminator" (William Burroughs), "During the Jurassic" (John Updike). [Monsters; Short stories]

482. Hitchcock, Alfred, ed. **Alfred Hitchcock's Monster Museum.** New York: Random House, 1965. 213pp. ISBN 0-394-84899-3. A

The "Master of the Macabre" selects some personal favorites, including "Slime" (Joseph Payne Brennan), "The King of the Cats" (Stephen Vincent Benet), "The Man Who Sold Rope to the Gnoles" (Idris Seabright), "Henry Martindale, Great Dane" (Miriam Allen deFord), "Shadow, Shadow on the Wall" (Theodore Sturgeon), "Doomsday Deferred" (Will F. Jenkins), "The Young One" (Jerome Bixby), "The Desrick on Yandro" (Manly Wade Wellman), "The Wheelbarrow Boy" (Richard Parker), "Homecoming" (Ray Bradbury). [Horror; Short stories]

483. Hitchcock, Alfred, ed. **Alfred Hitchcock's Supernatural Tales of Terror and Suspense.** New York: Random House, 1983. 213pp. ISBN 0-394-85622-8. A

Strange tales with mysterious elements woven into the plots include "Attention, Suspense Fans!," "The Triumph of Death" (H. Russell Wakefield), "The Strange Valley" (T. V. Olsen), "The Christmas Spirit" (Dorothy B. Bennett), "The Bronze Door" (Raymond Chandler), "Slip Stream" (Sheila Hodgson), "The Quest for 'Blank Cleveringi'" (Patricia Highsmith), "Miss Pinkerton's Apocalypse" (Muriel Spark), "The Reunion After Three Hundred Years" (Alexis Tolstoy), "The Attic Express" (Alex Hamilton), "The Pram" (A. W. Bennett), "Mr. Ash's Studio" (H. Russell Wakefield). [Horror; Short stories]

484. Hitchcock, Alfred, ed. **Alfred Hitchcock's Witch's Brew.** New York: Random House, 1983. 183pp. ISBN 0-394-85911-1. (First published by Random House, 1977). A

A nice mixture of terrible, nasty happenings, including "To Whet Your Appetite ...," "The Wishing Well" (E. F. Benson), "That Hell-Bound Train" (Robert Bloch), "As Gay As Cheese" (Joan Aiken), "Madame Mim" (T. H. White), "Blood Money" (M. Timothy O'Keefe), "His Coat So Gay" (Sterling Lanier), "They'll Never Find You Now" (Lord Dunsany), "In the Cards" (John Collier), "Strangers in Town" (Shirley Jackson), "The Proof" (John Moore). [Horror; Short stories]

485. Ireson, Barbara, ed. **Ghostly and Ghastly**. London: Beaver/Arrow, 1977. 222pp. ISBN 0-09-942710-9. **A**
    Other anthologies by Barbara Ireson: *Creepy Creatures; Fantasy Tales; Ghostly Laughter; Fearfully Frightening.*

Old and new favorites by English and American authors, including "The Emissary" (Ray Bradbury), "The Thing in the Cellar" (David H. Keller), "A Pair of Hands" (Sir Arthur Quiller-Couch), "The House of the Nightmare" (Edward Lucas White), "Miss Jemima" (Walter de la Mare), "The Devil's Cure" (Barbara Softly), "The Earlier Service" (Margaret Irwin), "Linda" (Joan Mahe), "Billy Bates' Story" (Geoffrey Palmer and Noel Lloyd), "Remembering Lee" (Eileen Bigland), "Jack-in-the-Box" (Ray Bradbury), "The Canterville Ghost" (Oscar Wilde). [Horror; Short stories]

486. Ireson, Barbara, ed. **Spooky Stories**. Ealing, England: Carousel, 1978- . **A**

Macabre stories by women writers. Stories in *Spooky Stories 6* include "Finders Keepers" (Joan Aiken), "Guess" (Philippa Pearce), "Witchcraft Unaware" (Rosemary Timperley), "The Figure" (Margaret Biggs), "Tea at Ravensburgh" (Joan Aiken), "The Empty Schoolroom" (Pamela Hansford Johnson), "The Girl in the Bedroom" (Margaret Biggs), "Can't Help Laughing" (Alison Prince). [Horror; Short stories]

487. Kahn, Joan, ed. **Some Things Strange and Sinister**. New York: Avon, 1973. 223pp. ISBN 0-380-0084-9. **A**
    Other compilations by the same editor: *Handle with Care; Frightening Stories; Some Things Dark and Dangerous.*

Some stories about unusual happenings, including "The Lamp" (Agatha Christie), "Nerves" (Guy de Maupassant), "Thus I Refute Beelzy" (John Collier), "Keeping His Promise" (Algernon Blackwood), "The House" (Andre Maurois), "The Call of the Hand" (Louis Golding), "The Dream Woman" (W. Wilkie Collins), "The Story of the Late Mr. Elvesham" (H. G. Wells), "The Strange Occurrences Connected with Captain John Russell" (Neil Bell), "The Book" (Margaret Irwin), "Dracula's Ghost" (Bram Stoker), "The Cocoon" (John B. L. Goodwin), "The Empty Schoolroom" (Pamela Hansford Johnson), "The Ghost of Washington" (Anonymous). [Horror; Short stories]

488. McCauley, Kirby, ed. **Dark Forces**. New York: Bantam, 1981. 544pp. ISBN 0-553-14801-X. **C**

Horror stories by contemporary writers, including "The Late Shift" (D. Etchison), "The Enemy" (I. B. Singer), "Dark Angel" (E. Bryant), "The Chest of Thirty-six" (D. Grubb), "Mark Ingestre: The Customer's Tale" (R. Aickman), "Where the Summer Ends" (K. E. Wagner), "The Bingo Master" (J. C. Oates), "Children of the Kingdom" (T. E. D. Klein), "The Detective of Dreams" (G. Wolfe), "Vengeance Is" (T. Sturgeon), "The Brood" (R. Campbell), "The Whistling Well" (C. D. Simak), "The Peculiar Demesne" (R. Kirk), "Where the Stones Grow" (T. Tuttle), "The Night Before Christmas" (R. Bloch), "The Stupid Joke" (E. Gorey), "A Touch of Petulance" (R. Bradbury), "Lindsay and the Red City Blues" (J. Haldeman), "A Garden of Blackred

Roses" (C. L. Grant), "Owls Hoot in the Daytime" (M. W. Wellman), "Where There's a Will" (R. Matheson and R. C. Matheson), "Traps" (G. Wilson), "The Mist" (S. King). [Horror; Short stories]

489. Molin, Charles, ed. **Ghosts, Spooks and Spectres**. Harmondsworth, England: Puffin, 1971. 185pp. ISBN 0-14-031485-7. (First published by Hamish Hamilton, 1967). **A**

A fine selection of various kinds of terror tales, including "Teeny-Tiny" (Anonymous), "The Signal-Man" (Charles Dickens), "The Strange Visitor" (Anonymous), "A Ghostly Wife" (Anonymous), "Legend of Hamilton Tighe" (Richard Bartram), "The Phantom Ship" (Captain Marryat), "The Brown Hand" (Sir Arthur Conan Doyle), "The Ghost-Brahman" (Anonymous), "The Ghost-Ship" (Richard Middleton), "The Water Ghost of Harrowby Hall" (John Kendrick Bangs), "The Inexperienced Ghost" (H. G. Wells), "The Buggane and the Tailor" (Dora Broome), "Laura" (Saki), "The Betrayal of Nance" (R. Blakeborough), "The Ghost Who Was Afraid of Being Bagged" (Anonymous), "The Beast with Five Fingers" (W. F. Harvey), "The Night the Ghost Got In" (James Thurber), "The Story of Glam" (Andrew Lang). [Ghosts; Short stories]

490. Morris, Janet, ed. **Heroes in Hell**. New York: Baen, 1986. 274pp. ISBN 0-671-65555-8. **C**

When people are bad enough to end up in Hell, this place can hardly be expected to be calm and tranquil. These stories of Hell include "Son of the Morning" (Chris Morris), "Newton Sleep" (Gregory Benford), "The Prince" (C. J. Cherryh), "A Walk in the Park" (Nancy Asire), "The Hand of Providence" (David Drake), "Basileus" (C. J. Cherryh and Janet Morris), "To Reign in Hell" (Janet Morris). [Hell; Short stories]

491. Morris, Janet, ed. **Rebels in Hell**. New York: Baen, 1986. 308pp. ISBN 0-621-65577-9. **C**

Stories of the bad, who never stop trying, including "Undercover Agent" (Chris Morris), "Hell's Gate" (Bill Kerby), "Gilgamesh in the Outback" (Robert Silverberg), "Marking Time" (C. J. Cherryh), "Table with a View" (Nancy Asire), "There Are No Fighter Pilots Down in Hell" (Martin Caidin), " 'Cause I Served My Time in Hell' " (David Drake), "Monday Morning" (C. J. Cherryh), "Graveyard Shift" (Janet Morris). [Hell; Short stories]

492. **The [numbered] Pan Book of Horror Stories**. London: Pan, 1959- . **A**

Over twenty collections have been published to date. These stories may seem gentle at first, but when you think about them .... Book number 13 includes "The Man Whose Nose Was Too Big" (Alan Hillery), "Flame!" (Norman Kaufman), "The Twins" (Harry Turner), "The Swans" (Carl Thomson), "The Revenge" (David Farrer), "Window Watcher" (Dulcie Gray), "Spinalonga" (John Ware), "Aggrophobia" (L. Micallef), "Awake, Sleeping Tigress" (Norman Kaufman), "The Dead End" (David Case). [Horror; Short stories]

493.   Salmonson, Jessica Amanda, ed. **Tales by Moonlight**. New York: TOR, 1983. 286pp. ISBN 0-812-52552-3. **C**

An uneven collection with some really fine stories. Introduced by Stephen King, the stories include "The Nocturnal Visitor" (Dale C. Donaldson), "Flames" (Jeffrey Lant), "An Egg for Ava" (Richard Lee-Fulgham), "See the Station Master" (George Florance-Guthridge), "A Tulip for Eulie" (Austelle Pool), "Cobwebs" (Jody Scott), "The Toymaker and the Musicrafter" (Phyllis Ann Karr), "Witches" (Janet Fox), "A Night Out" (Nina Kiriki Hoffman), "Jaborandi Jazz" (Gordon Linzner), "A Wine of Heart's Desire" (Ron Nance), "Spring Conditions" (Eileen Gunn), "The Sky Came Down to Earth" (Steve Rasnic Tem), "Joan" (Mary Ann Allen), "The Night of the Red, Red Moon" (Elinor Busby), "Toyman's Name" (Phyllis Ann Karr), "Dog Killer" (William H. Green), "The Mourning After" (Bruce McDonald), "The Hill Is No Longer There" (John D. Berry), "The Inhabitant of the Pond" (Linda Thornton). [Horror; Short stories]

494.   Shepard, Leslie, ed. **The Dracula Book of Great Horror Stories**. Secaucus, N. J.: Citadel, 1981. 288pp. ISBN 0-8065-0765-9. **C**
Other anthologies: *The Dracula Book of Great Vampire Stories.*

Classic tales by the all-time great writers, including "Captain Murderer" (Charles Dickens), "The Pit and the Pendulum" (Edgar Allan Poe), "The Haunted and the Haunters: or, The House and the Brain" (Sir Edward Bulwer-Lytton), "The Inn" (Guy De Maupassant), "The Dancing Partner" (Jerome K. Jerome), "The Cone" (H. G. Wells), "The Monkey's Paw" (W. W. Jacobs), "Caterpillars" (E. F. Benson), "The Judge's House" (Bram Stoker), "The Voice in the Night" (W. H. Hodgson), "The Festival" (H. P. Lovecraft), "County Magnus" (M. R. James), "The Travelling Grave" (L. P. Hartley), "The Wendigo" (A. Blackwood). [Horror; Short stories]

495.   Singer, Kurt, ed. **The [numbered] Target Book of Horror**. London: Target, 1983?- . **A**

Timeless tales of terror and fear. Contents of book two include "The Man Who Cried Wolf!" (Robert Bloch), "The Nameless Mummy" (Arlton Eadie), "The Man They Couldn't Hang" (Judge Marcus Kavanagh), "Legal Rites" (Isaac Asimov and James MacCreagh), "The Devil and Sharon Tate" (Michael Ballantine), "The Exorcist—New York Style" (Kurt and Jane Singer), "Not According to Dante" (Malcolm Jameson).
Contents of book four include "The Haunted and the Haunters" (Lord Lytton), "The 'Ouanga' Charm" (W. B. Seabrook), "Green Jewel of Death" (Princess Catherine Radziwill), "The Phantom Coach" (Elma B. Edwards), "Ghosts Come to Hell" (Pat Scholer), "Wages of Envy" (Mark Bartholomeusz), "White Lady of the Hohenzollerns" (Clyde Clark). [Horror; Short stories]

496.   Summers, Montague, ed. **The Penguin Supernatural Omnibus**. Harmondsworth, England: Penguin, 1976. 573pp. ISBN 0-14-00-7297-7. (First published by Victor Gollancz, 1931). **C**

A weighty collection of mysterious stories, collected by a mysterious occult personage, including "Narrative of the Ghost of a Hand" (J. Sheridan Le Fanu), "An Account of Some Strange Disturbances in Aungier Street" (J. Sheridan Le Fanu), "Man-size in Marble" (Evelyn Nesbit), "The Judge's House" (Bram Stoker), "Perceval Landon" (Thurnley Abbey), "The Story of the Spaniards" (E. and H. Heron), "The Phantom Coach" (Amelia B. Edwards), "Brickett Bottom" (Amyas Northcote), "The Cold Embrace" (Miss Braddon), "How the Third Floor Knew the Potteries" (Amelia B. Edwards), "Not to Be Taken at Bed-time" (Rosa Mulholland), "To Be Taken with a Grain of Salt" (Charles Dickens), "The Signal-man" (Charles Dickens), "The Compensation House" (Charles Collins), "The Engineer" (Amelia B. Edwards), "When I was Dead" (Vincent O'Sullivan), "The Story of Yand Manor House" (E. and H. Heron), "The Business of Madame Jahn" (Vincent O'Sullivan), "Amour Dure" (Vernon Lee), "Oke of Okehurst" (Vernon Lee), "Eveline's Visitant" (Miss Braddon), "John Charrington's Wedding" (Evelyn Nesbit), "De Profundis" (Roger Pater), "The Dream Woman" (Wilkie Collins), "Singular Passage in the Life of the Late Henry Harris, Doctor in Divinity" (Richard Barham), "The Spirit of Stonehenge" (Jasper John), "The Seeker of Souls" (Jasper John), "The Astrologer's Legacy" (Roger Pater), "My Brother's Ghost Story" (Amelia B. Edwards), "Sir Dominick's Bargain" (J. Sheridan Le Fanu), "The Bargain of Rupert Orange" (Vincent O'Sullivan), "Carmilla" (J. Sheridan Le Fanu), "The White Wolf of the Hartz Mountains" (Frederick Marryat), "A Porta Inferi" (Roger Pater), "Jerry Jarvis's Wig" (Richard Barham), "The Watcher o' the Dead" (John Guinan), "The Story of Konnor Old House" (E. and H. Heron), "Toussel's Bride" (W. B. Seabrook). [Short stories]

497.   Wagner, Karl Edward, ed. **The Year's Best Horror Stories**. New York: Daw, 1972- . C
        Series I-III edited by Richard Davis; Series IV-VII edited by Gerald Page, Series VIII- edited by Karl Edward Wagner.

Good selections of stories selected by an expert in the field. Contents of Series XIV (1986) include: "Penny Daye" (Charles L. Grant), "Dwindling" (David B. Silva), "Dead Men's Fingers" (Phillip C. Heath), "Dead Week" (Leonard Carpenter), "The Sneering" (Ramsey Campbell), "Bunny Didn't Tell Us" (David J. Schow), "Pinewood" (Tanith Lee), "The Night People" (Michael Reaves), "Ceremony" (William F. Nolan), "The Woman in Black" (Dennis Etchison), "... Beside the Seaside, Beside the Sea ..." (Simon Clark), "Mother's Day" (Stephen F. Wilcox), "Lava Tears" (Vincent McHardy), "Rapid Transit" (Wayne Allen Sallee), "The Weight of Zero" (John Alfred Taylor), "John's Return to Liverpool" (Christopher Burns), "In Late December, before the Storm" (Paul M. Sammon), "Red Christmas" (David S. Garnett), "Too Far behind Gradina" (Steve Sneyd). [Horror; Short stories]

498.   Waugh, Carol-Lynn Rossel, Martin Harry Greenberg, and Isaac Asimov, eds. **13 Horrors of Halloween**. New York: Avon, 1983. 175pp. ISBN 0-380-81814-7. A

Stories for that most magical night of the year, including "Halloween" (Isaac Asimov), "Unholy Hybrid" (William Bankier), "Trick-or-Treat" (Anthony Boucher), "The October Game" (Ray Bradbury), "Halloween Girl" (Robert Grant), "Day of the Vampire" (Edward D. Hoch), "Night of the Goblin" (Talmage Powell), "The Adventure of the Dead Cat" (Ellery Queen), "Pumpkin Head" (Al Sarrantonio), "The Circle" (Lewis Shiner), "All Souls' " (Edith Wharton), "Yesterday's Witch" (Gahan Wilson), "Victim of the Year" (Robert F. Young). [Short stories]

499. Wilson, Gahan, ed., **Favorite Tales of Horror**. New York: Tempo, 1976. 186pp. ISBN 0-448-12627-3. **A**

Noted cartoonist and critic of horror books and movies edits a collection of tales for teens, including "Kitty Fisher" (Charles Birkin), "The Treader of the Dust" (Clark Ashton Smith), "The Horror of the Heights" (Sir Arthur Conan Doyle), "The Sea Was Wet as Wet Could Be" (Gahan Wilson), "Luella Miller" (Mary Wilkins Freeman), "The Idol with Hands of Clay" (Sir Frederick Treves), "My Favorite Murder" (Ambrose Bierce), "The Clock" (William Fryer Harvey), "The Harbor-Master" (Robert W. Chambers), "Rats" (M. R. James). [Ghosts; Short stories]

500. Windling, Terri, ed. **Faery!** New York: Ace Science Fiction, 1985. 308pp. ISBN 0-441-22564-0. **C**

A collection of charming stories about the strange inhabitants of the shadowy secret world of inhuman beings, including "A Troll and Two Roses" (Patricia A. McKillip), "The Thirteenth Fey" (Jane Yolen), "Lullaby for a Changeling" (Nicholas Stuart Gray), "Brat" (Theodore Sturgeon), "Wild Garlic" (William F. Wu), "The Stranger" (Shulamith Oppenheim), "Spirit Places" (Keith Taylor), "The Box of All Possibility" (Z. Greenstaff), "The Seekers of Dreams" (Felix Marti-Ibanez), "Bridge" (Steven R. Boyett), "Crowley and the Leprechaun" (Gregory Frost), "The Antrim Hills" (Mildred Downey Broxon), "The Snow Fairy" (M. Lucie Chin), "The Five Black Swans" (Sylvia Townsend Warner), "Thomas the Rhymer" (Traditional Scots Ballad), "Prince Shadowbow" (Sheri S. Tepper), "The Erlking" (Angela Carter), "The Elphin Knight" (Traditional Scots Ballad), "Rhian and Garanhir" (Grail Undwin), "The Woodcutter's Daughter" (Alison Uttley), "The Famous Flower of Serving Men" (Traditional Scots Ballad), "Touk's House" (Robin McKinley), "The Boy Who Dreamed of Tir Na N-og" (Michael M. McNamara). [Fairies; Short stories]

Part 3
Appendices

Books in Series

Books in series are listed in the publisher's numbered series order. Not all titles are annotated earlier.

Dark Forces Series, 1983- .

Published by Bantam, New York. A series dealing with the dark side of occult themes. Written for teens with strong stomachs. **A**

Logan, Les. *The Game.*

Bridges, Laurie, and Paul Alexander. *Magic Show.*

Sparger, Rex. *The Doll.*

Bridges, Laurie, and Paul Alexander. *Devil Wind.*

Sparger, Rex. *The Bargain.*

Bridges, Laurie, and Paul Alexander. *Swamp Witch.*

Logan, Les. *Unnatural Talent.*

Siegel, Scott. *The Companion.*

Coville, Bruce. *Eyes of the Tarot.*

Siegel, Scott. *Beat the Devil.*

Coville, Bruce. *Waiting Spirits.*

Bridges, Laurie. *The Ashton Horror.*

Weinburg, Larry. *The Curse.*

Scott, R. C. *Blood Sports.*

Polcovar, Jane. *The Charming.*

ESP McGee Series, 1983- .

A series for younger teens with each book about a young hero with paranormal abilities. **B**

Packard, Edward. *ESP McGee.*

Lawrence, Jim. *ESP McGee and the Haunted Mansion.*

Ernst, Kathryn F. *ESP McGee and the Mysterious Magician.*

Rodger, Jesse. *ESP and the Dolphin's Message.*

Shea, George. *ESP McGee to the Rescue.*

Find Your Fate Series, 1984- .

These books provide a choice of endings. They are based on the character of Indiana Jones from the hit movies. The reader makes decisions for Indiana along the way of each adventure. They are written for younger teens and published by Ballantine. **B**

Stine, Robert L. *Indiana Jones and the Curse of Horror Island.*

Estes, Rose. *Indiana Jones and the Lost Treasure of Sheba.*

Stine, Robert L. *Indiana Jones and the Giants of the Silver Tower.*

Wende, Richard. *Indiana Jones and the Eye of the Fates.*

Helfer, Andrew. *Indiana Jones and the Cup of the Vampires.*

Wenk, Richard. *Indiana Jones and the Legion of Death.*

Stine, Robert L. *Indiana Jones and the Cult of the Mummy's Crypt.*

Stine, Megan, and H. William Stine. *Indiana Jones and the Dragon of Vengeance.*

Weiss, Ellen. *Indiana Jones and the Gold of Genghis Khan.*

Twilight Series, 1982- .

Published by Dell, New York. A series of books for teens dealing with occult themes. Less gruesome than the Dark Forces series. **A**

Cowan, Dale. *Deadly Sleep.*

Haynes, Betsy. *The Power.*

Brunn, Robert. *The Initiation.*

Howe, Imogen. *Fatal Attraction.*

Francis, Dorothy Brenner. *Blink of the Mind.*

Haynes, James. *Voices in the Dark.*

Veley, Charles. *Play to Live.*

Armstrong, Sarah. *Blood Red Roses.*

Daniel, Colin. *Demon Tree.*

Stevenson, E. *The Avenging Spirit.*

Laymon, Carl. *Nightmare Lake.*

Smith, Janet Patton. *The Twisted Room.*

Howe, Imogen. *Vicious Circle.*

Callahan, Jay. *Footprints of the Dead.*

Coville, Bruce. *Spirits & Spells.*

Selden, Neil. *Drawing the Dead.*

Netter, Susan. *Storm Child.*

Trainor, Joseph. *Watery Grave.*

Kassem, Lou. *Dance of Death.*

Trainor, Joseph. *Family Crypt.*

Cusick, Richie Tankersley. *Evil on the Bayou.*

Blake, Susan. *The Haunted Dollhouse.*

Bryan, Amanda. *The Warning.*

Coville. *Amulet of Doom.*

Gonzalez, Gloria. *A Deadly Rhyme.*

The Zodiac Club, 1984- .

Published by Pacer/Berkley, New York. A series for teens, the stories of female protagonists deal mainly with romance. Astrology plays a part in all the books, since the young heroines are members of an astrology club. **B**

Daniels, Gail. *The Stars Unite.*

Godfrey, Sarah. *Aries Rising.*

Nichols, Lynn J. *Taurus Trouble.*

Rees, E. M. *Libra's Dilemma.*

Palatini, Margie. *Capricorn & Co.*

Kroll, Joanna. *Sagittarius Serving.*

Lawrence, S. J. *Aquarius Ahoy!*

Rees, E. M. *Gemini Solo.*

Daniels, Gail. *Cancer, the Moonchild.*

Rees, E. M. *Pisces Times Two.*

Palatini, Margie. *Scorpio's Class Act.*

Movie List

Numbers following the titles refer to entry number.

Directory of Paperback Publishers

Publishers' addresses and distribution centers change frequently, so it is best to doublecheck information in current listings of publishers in sources such as *Books in Print*.

Academy Chicago
425 N. Michigan Ave.
Chicago, IL 60611

Ace Books. *See* Berkley

Ace Charter. *See* Berkley

Ace Fantasy. *See* Berkley

Ace Science Fiction. *See* Berkley

Airmont Publishing Company
401 Lafayette Sq.
New York, NY 10003

Aladdin Press
Harvard St., Ste 10
Brookline, MA 02146

Arbor House
235 E. 45th St.
New York, NY 10017

Archway. *See* Washington Square

Armada
8 Grafton St.
London, WIX 3LA
England

Armada/Fontana. *See* Armada

Arrow Books
17-21 Conway St.
London, W1P 6JD
England

Avon
1790 Broadway
New York, NY 10019

Avon/Bard. *See* Avon

Avon/Camelot. *See* Avon

Avon/Flare. *See* Avon

Award Books
Spring House
Spring House Place
London, NW5 3BH
England

Baen Publishing Enterprises
260 Fifth Ave. Ste. 35
New York, NY 10001

Ballantine
201 E. 50th St.
New York, NY 10022

Ballantine/Del Rey. *See* Ballantine

Bantam Books
666 5th Ave.
New York, NY 10017

Bantam/Skylark. *See* Bantam

Bantam/Spectra. *See* Bantam

Beaver/Arrow
15605 N.W. Cornell Rd.
Beaverton, OR 97006

Berkley Publishers
200 Madison Ave.
New York, NY 10016

Calder Ltd.
18 Brewer St.
London, W1R 4AS
England

Canongate Publishers
17 Jeffrey St.
Edinburgh, EH1 1DR
Scotland

Carroll & Graf
260 Fifth Ave.
New York, NY 10001

Centaur
799 Broadway
New York, NY 10003

Charterhouse
3 W. 57th St.
New York, NY 10019

Citadel
120 Enterprise Ave.
Secaucus, NJ 079094

Continuum
370 Lexington Ave.
New York, NY 10017

Corgi
61-63 Uxbridge Rd.
Ealing
London, W5 5SA
England

Critics' Choice Paperbacks
31 E. 28th St.
New York, NY 10016

Daw Books
1633 Broadway
New York, NY 10019

Day. *See* Stein and Day

Dell Publishing Company
1 Dag Hammarskjold Plaza
245 E. 47th St.
New York, NY 10017

Dell/Yearling. *See* Dell

Delta. *See* Dell

Dover Publications
31 E. Second St.
Mineola, NY 11501

Eerdmans
255 Jefferson Ave., S.E.
Grand Rapids, MI 49503

Emerald/Dell. *See* Dell

Fawcett
201 E. 50th St.
New York, NY 10022

Fawcett/Crest. *See* Fawcett

Fontana Lions. *See* Armada

Hippo
10 Earlham St.
London, WC2H 9LN
England

Jove. *See* Berkley

Knight
Tolley House
17 Scarbrook Rd.
Croydon, CRO 15Q
England

Lancer Books
1560 Broadway
New York, NY 10036

Laurel-Leaf. *See* Dell

Leisure Books
6 E. 39th St.
New York

Lorevan. *See* Critics' Choice

Magnet
11 New Fretter Ln.
London, EC4P 4EE
England

Meridian Publishers
2643 Edgewood Rd.
Utica, NY 13501

NAL
New American Library
1633 Broadway
New York, NY 10019

Newcastle Publishers
13149 Saticoy St.
North Hollywood, CA 91605

Pacer/Berkley. *See* Berkley

Pan
Cavayne Place
London, SW10 9PG
England

Panther
8 Grafton St.
London, W1X 3LA
England

Paperback Library. *See* Warner
        Books

Penguin
40 W. 23rd St.
New York, NY 10010

Perigee
200 Madison Ave.
New York, NY 10016

Pinnacle Books
1430 Broadway
New York, NY 10018

Playboy Paperbacks
200 Madison Ave.
New York, NY 10019

Plume. *See* New American Library

Pocket Books. *See* Washington Square

Popular Library Books
666 5th Ave.
New York, NY 10103
(Acquired by Warner and
        discontinued)

Puffin. *See* Penguin

Puffin Plus. *See* Penguin

Pyramid
919 Third Ave.
New York, NY 10022

Random House
201 E. 50th St.
New York, NY 10022

Scholastic Inc.
730 Broadway
New York, NY 10003

Scholastic/Apple. *See* Scholastic
        Inc.

Scholastic/Point. *See* Scholastic
        Inc.

Signet. *See* New American Library

Spectra. *See* Bantam

Sphere
30-32 Gray's Inn Rd.
London, WC1X 8JL
England

Star Books
44 Hill St.
London, W1X 8LB
England

Stein and Day
Scarborough House
Briarcliff Manor, NY 10510

Target. *See* Star

Tempo
200 Madison Ave.
New York, NY 10016

TOR Books
49 W. 24th St.
New York, NY 10010

Trophy
Harper & Row
10 East 53rd St.
New York, NY 10022

Vintage. *See* Random House

Wanderer
Division of Simon & Schuster
1230 Avenue of the Americas
New York, NY 10020

Warner Books
666 Fifth Ave.
New York, NY 10103

Washington Square/Pocket Books
1230 Avenue of the Americas
New York, NY 10020

Woodhill
300 W. 43rd St.
New York, NY 10036

Workman
One West 39th St.
New York, NY 10018

Zebra
475 Park Ave. S.
New York, NY 10016

Zebra/Kensington. *See* Zebra

Zephyr
245 Park Ave.
New York, NY 10017

Title Index

Reference is to entry number.

Subject Index

Reference is to entry number.